WHEEL AND COME AGAIN

WHEEL AND COME AGAIN

AN ANTHOLOGY OF REGGAE POETRY

SELECTED BY KWAME DAWES

PEEPAL TREE

First published in 1998
and reprinted with biographical updates in 2008
Peepal Tree Press Ltd
17 King's Avenue
Leeds LS6 1QS

ISBN 1 900715 13 9
ISBN 13: 9781900715133

ARTS COUNCIL
ENGLAND   Peepal Tree gratefully acknowledges Arts Council support

ACKNOWLEDGEMENTS

The editor and publishers would like to thank the following for their kind permission to use their poems in this anthology:
John Agard c/o Caroline Sheldon Literary Agency for 'For Bob Marley'; Lillian Allen for 'Riddim An' Hardtimes' and 'Rubba Dub Style Inna Regent Park' from *Women Do This Every Day*, Toronto, Ontario, Women's Press, 1993; Edward Baugh for 'Nigger Sweat' from *A Tale From the Rainforest*, Sandberry Press, 1988; James Berry and Bloodaxe Books for 'Sounds of a Dreamer' from *Hot Earth Cold Earth*, Bloodaxe, 1995; Marion Bethel for 'Reggae Prophecy' from *Guanahani, Mi Amor*, Casa de las Americas, 1994; Kamau Brathwaite for 'Stone: for Mikey Smith' from *Jah Music*, Savacou Publications, 1986; Jean Binta Breeze for 'Riddym Ravings', 'Eena Mi Corner' and 'Dubbed Out' from *Riddym Ravings and Other Poems*, Race Today Publications, 1988; Stewart Brown for 'Let Them Call It Jazz'; Afua Cooper for 'Stepping To Da Muse/Sic' from *Memories Have Tongue*, Sistervision, 1992; Fred D'Aguiar and Bloodaxe Books for 'Dread' and 'GDR' from *British Subjects*, Bloodaxe Books, 1993 and Chatto and Windus for 'Dreadtalk' from *Mama Dot*, Chatto and Windus, 1985; Ramabhai Espinet and Sistervision for 'Merchant of Death' from *Nuclear Seasons*, Sistervision Press, 1991; Lorna Goodison for 'For Don Drummond' from *Tamarind Season*, Institute of Jamaica, 1980, 'Jah Music' from *I am Becoming My Mother*, New Beacon, 1986; 'Upon a Quarter Million' and 'Heartease III from *Heartease*, New Beacon, 1989; Audrey Ingram Roberts for 'Poem II' published in *Creation Fire*, Sistervision Press, 1990; Linton Kwesi Johnson and LKJ Records Ltd for 'Bass Culture', 'Reggae Sounds' and 'Five Nights of Bleeding' from *Dread Beat and Blood*, Bogle L'Ouverture 1975; Jane King and Sandberry Press for 'Intercity Dub' from *Fellow Traveller*, Sandberry Press; Malachi for 'Psalm of Silk'; The estate of Anthony McNeill and Savacou Publications for 'Saint Ras', 'Ode to Brother Joe', 'For the D' from *Reel from 'The Life Movie'*, 1972 and to the Institute of Jamaica for 'Bob Marley: New King of the Music' from *Credences at The Altar of Sound*, 1979; Ahdri Zhina Mandiela for 'Mih Feel It' and 'Special Rikwes' from *Special Rikwes*, Toronto, 199?; Mbala (Michael Bailey) for 'A New Dub' and 'The History of Dub Poetry'; Brian Meeks and Savacou Publications for 'The Twin Barrel Bucky: A Kingston 12 Dub', 'Is Culcha Weapon?' and 'March 9, 1976' first published in *Savacou 14/15: New Poets From Jamaica;* Pam Mordecai for 'Jesus is Condemned to Death' from *De Man*, Sandberry

Press; Mervyn Morris and New Beacon Books for 'Valley Prince', 'Rasta Reggae' from *The Pond*, New Beacon, 1973and 'For Consciousness' from *Shadow Boxing*, New Beacon, 1979; Grace Nichols and Virago Press for 'Beverley's Saga' from *Lazy Thoughts of a Lazy Woman*, Virago, 1989; Opal Adisa Palmer and Sistervision Press for 'No, Women Don't Cry', 'Ethiopia Under a Mango Tree' and 'Count Ossie' from *Tamarind and Mango Women*, 1992; Rohan Preston and Tia Chucha Press for 'Music', 'Italist Chant', 'Deep Sea Bathing', Champion Chant' and 'Ten Seconds' from *Dreams in Soy Sauce*, Tia Chucha Press, 1992; Mrs Joy Scott, executor for the estate of Dennis Scott and New Beacon Books for 'Apocalypse Dub', 'Dreadwalk' and 'More Poem' from *Dreadwalk*, New Beacon Books, 1982; Olive Senior and Bloodaxe Books for 'Meditation on Yellow' from *Gardening in the Tropics*, Bloodaxe, 1995; Vejay Steede for 'Reggae'; Norman Weinstein and Mellen Poetry Press for 'Drummond's Lover Sings the Blues', 'Garvey's Head as Value', 'The Ethiopian Apocalypse of Don' and 'The Migration of Drummond's Organs (After Death' from *Suite: Orchid Ska Blues*, Mellen Poetry Press.

Sources of poems by authors published by Peepal Tree Press: Kwame Dawes, 'Trickster I', 'Trickster II' and 'Trickster IV' from *Jacko Jacobus*, 1996, 'Some Tentative Definitions I, IV, VII and IX' and 'Black Heart' are from *Shook Foil: A Collection of Reggae Poems, 1997;* Kendel Hippolyte, 'Revo Lyric', 'Jah-Son/Another Way', 'Reggae Cat', 'Antonette's Boogie' and 'So Jah Sey' are from *Birthright*, 1997; Rachel Manley, 'Bob Marley's Dead' is from *A Light Left On*, 1992; Marc Matthews, 'By A Ways' and 'Language' are from *A Season of Sometimes*, 1992; Geoffrey Philp 'Heirlooms' and 'Dance Hall' are from *Florida Bound*, 1995, 'Dance Hall:Version' and 'One Song' are from *Hurricane Center*, 1998; Velma Pollard 'Heaven's Cherubim High Horsed or The Meeting of the Two Sevens' is from *Shame Trees Don't Grow Here... but poincianas bloom*, 1992.

The editor and publishers were unable to trace Bongo Jerry whose 'Mabrak' appeared in *Savacou 3/ 4*; Dorothy Wong Loi Sing whose 'Baap Nesmesthe Reggae Son' appeared in *Creation Fire*, 1990; the executors of the late Lloyd Richardson whose 'The Poet Sings His Painting' appeared in *Savacou 14/15*; and Bob Stewart whose 'August Town' and 'Words Is Not Enough' appeared in *Cane Cut*, Savacou Co-operative, 1988.

CONTENTS

COLIN CHANNER

PREFACE

Wheel & Come Again is Caribbean poetry's boomshot tribute to reggae music. Ambitious in scope and impressive in execution, *Wheel* is more than a collection of clear-eyed writing. It's a gun salute, a loud pram-pram, an echoing bawl of fah-wud supporting the idea that reggae is vital and valid as a literary model. There is a lot to celebrate here. Seeing the work of newer writers such as the unfairly gifted Rohan Preston cotched against that of an enduring writer such as Olive Senior is reason to roll a spliff. But can we call it an anthology? And should we even want to? That's a question we need to ask. For, working like a selector on a heavyweight sound, cutting and mixing with experienced fingers, Dawes has created not an overview, not a survey, but something new and exciting that demands a bolder definition.

But what though? We're not sure yet. And that's a part of the excitement. A great deal of it is textual – a fair expectation after a prip at the table of contents. Lorna Goodison. Anthony McNeill. Jean Breeze. Mervyn Morris. Fred D'Aguiar. But a heapa it is textural, a point that becomes rachet sharp after penetrating this – that Dawes, without winking, nodding, or holding out his hand for a snare-slap high five, has found a way to blend into the mix, without breaking the groove, the work of younger, less well-known poets; poets whose contribution in the 70s is in danger of being forgotten; as well as poets whose connection to the roots tradition, as either influence or practitioner, has to this point been overlooked. That is the bigness of the collection – we still haven't found the right word yet – it brings us the kind of fresh vision and expanded judgement more readily associated with a sip off a chalice filled to the brim with just-cut, slow-burning, green sensimilla, the kind we Jamaicans keep a-yard when we send off de plane to farrin.

And it's here I believe the answer lurks. (Again, what should we call this thing?) It lies in the compressed spaces between the work. For like the realisation that confronts Jamaicans as they simmer in traffic, wet with the heat of the sun – banker next to barrister, clerk behind courier – there's an overarching framework that unites them despite the class divisions and social fissures that threaten to split the Rock into a loose association of fiefdoms ruled by corrupt politicians, ruffneck drug lords and cliché spouting lecturers at the university. The framework is reggae, a form as strong and supple as bamboo. From the blues-reactive solos of ska to dancehall's rap-shaping chatter, reggae is the soul force of the Jamaican body politic. It has influenced the arts as well, bubbling beneath the canvases of painters such as Osmond Watson, and has chopped away the mento-minded doggedness of the National Dance Theatre Company. Literature, to this point, has been the last redoubt, the last of the genres to surrender to the avant-garde of Jah's army.

Luckily we have in Dawes a blessed trinity, a Ph. D. in literature, an award-winning poet and a former lead-singer with a reggae band – in other words an egghead with a rasta tam to weave together for us with the skill and care of a dub organiser – a Scratch Perry, a King Tubby, a Prince Jammy – not some tweedy compilation (we still can't find the word to describe it), a spiralling freefall through the cross-faded currents of the Caribbean poetic impulse, from high-hat writers to the melting bottom of a one-drop groove…

But what should we call this book which we hold in our hands, this collection of thought and expression that threatens to bend the establishment's face like a brandished McAbee version? Testament? Eulogy? Ode?

The publishers say it's an anthology. They have to say this. This is the language that the bookstores understand. But calling this an anthology is like referring to Marley's crown of thorns as a hair style. What is it? The answer, we said earlier, is hiding between those compressed spaces.

So read this book slowly. Sit in a soft chair in good light. Stop
and think as you cross those spaces. And when you're through,
write a letter to the publisher and tell them what to call this...

Colin Channer
London, U.K.
October 1, 1997
(Delroy Wilson on the CD player singing "I'm Still Waiting")

KWAME DAWES

INTRODUCTION

The signal snap of the snare drum – a tight snare, almost metallic the way the stick cracks it, the rim ringing – it is not quite a roll, it is too tight, too short for that, but it is the announcement of the coming of the drum kick that holds back just long enough – waiting for the three, between the eighths of the stammering high-hat – just long enough to let the feel of a drop take you. It booms steady like a predictable hiccup – it always comes just after you expect. The bass guitar guarantees a melody as sweetly seductive as it is deadly serious – a true anchor. You can't understand the crucial importance of the drum and bass until you gut a reggae song and study the slippery viscera of its exposed innards. The bass is not just the frame, the skeleton; it is the heart beating, the engine, the intelligence. Without it the whole thing crumbles, becomes inert and lifeless. When the syncopations of the bubbling keyboards, with their inverted percussive hops, enter the fray, your body, if it is anything like mine, is grinning with recognition, with a sense of satisfaction and expectation. There is a filling of the vacuum – it is what Kendel Hippolyte is talking about in 'Antonette's Boogie':

> right in the middle of the song
> Bob singing stop – de rams' horns start to wail
> and dis dance-hall is an ark
> dis dance become a journey

Reggae is about spaces, about the way sound fills space and then vacates space to create the suggestion of energy.

When I listen to reggae, my mind sifts through a complex of memories labelled by a mood, a cadence, a quality of sound that evokes a world of experience. I can sniff out a reggae song from a remarkable distance. I do it quickly, effectively, and I find myself gravitating towards the sound, always. Reggae is a staple in my diet. This is a simple fact. The only thing that bothers me is an anxiety about whether I am alone in this. I know that Bob Marley understood what I feel when a snare kicks in the tune. Look at any footage of him on stage, his head thrown back, his arms stretched out crucifixion-style, his body almost completely still, except for this peculiar waving of his torso as if he is being washed by waves of sound, transfixed by the grounding of his music which touches everything in him. And by this stillness, with the hint of undulation, you can tell that he has entered a place where the rhythm is in complete control. It is a place of sweetness, a spot in a groove that is perfectly comfortable, perfectly right. There is nothing like it. It is the same quality you can see in some women on the dance floor. She looks down at a spot before her feet, her face stern with concentration and her body walking back and forth on the spot. She is talking to herself, reaching into herself, she is shaped by the music. A poem, a poem. This is the taste of reggae — it emerges in the way people move to it.

I am sure that not everyone feels like this and, perhaps, short of becoming a reggae singer and touring like Marley did and Burning Spear does, as a minstrel or ambassador of this music, all that is open to me, as I am driven to do, is to write poems which try to capture the poetry of this music in a way which might communicate to others. When I played in a reggae band, I discovered the poetry of being a singer on stage while a tight band rolls out reggae song after reggae song. It is a powerful thing that you never get over. But I have been a poet for a long time, and I have this strange faith in the capacity of the poem to capture the spirit of a moment. It may be that the poem is the only form that can capture the non-linearity of the reggae song, the layered construction, and the multidimensional pattern of its meanings and concerns. But the poem cannot stand in the place of the reggae song — as I think that some of writing labelled 'dub poetry' tends to do. Instead, the poem must try and capture the spirit of reggae in its own terms as poetry, using all the resources of poetry. I think this is what many of the poets collected here are attempting to do. They are dialoguing with the reggae song even as they are trying to replicate its spirit in their poems. This anthology contains a long list of poets whose poems, they hope, will somehow awake in the reader the same reaction to the music that I have described. What has emerged are not reggae songs (without the music and fire of performance) but a new poetic fired by the reggae mood, the reggae intelligence and the reggae aesthetic.

It was the simplicity and depth of Marley's lyrics that filled me with fascination and envy. The cleverly achieved contradictions – spiritual candour and almost evangelical zeal with the most natural and frank of sexual expression; the absurdist humour with the dire brutality of political reckoning; the esoteric with the populist; the rough with the sublime – these things coming together in the most persuasive way offered me a model of poetic grace and genius that was enviable and deeply tempting. This is what Vejay Steede's breakneck celebration/definition of reggae reveals. Reggae is a multiplicity of things that are brought together in a dynamic fashion, a distinctive fashion.

It is inevitable that Marley stands out as the reggae poet whose posture, whose entire oeuvre and whose life fascinates the creative artists of the Caribbean. The number of poems that celebrate Marley's life and music in this collection exemplify this fascination. Derek Walcott speaking on a BBC programme some years ago selected two Marley songs; "No Woman No Cry" and "Redemption Song" among eight songs he loved greatly. He praised the sincerity of Marley's lyrics and his capacity to capture the conditions of the working class in direct and evocative language. Always, though, at the edges of Walcott's statement was a sense of a class divide between his imagination and Marley's. It is a typical West Indian problem that reggae somehow complicates. Before reggae, it was possible for writers working in Jamaica to speak of themselves as spokespersons for what George Lamming called the peasant experience. It was possible for H.G. Delisser to treat *Jane's Career* (1914) as an excursion into the exotic world of the working class Jamaican, or for Victor Reid in *New Day* (1949) to seek to connect with a peasant language and ethos in the telling of a political tale of independence. It was possible for Roger Mais to be celebrated as a writer who had entered the "seedy underbelly" of Kingston and emerged with poetic novels like *The Hills Were Joyful Together* (1953) and *Brother Man* (1954). This pattern is reflected in the sociological novels of Orlando Patterson (*The Children of Sisyphus,* 1964 and *An Absence of Ruins*, 1967) and in the early work of Andrew Salkey (*A Quality of Violence*, 1959) and Sylvia Wynter (*The Hills of Hebron*, 1962). These writers were serious about speaking for the voiceless because they had concluded that it was in the world of this voiceless mass that the true Jamaican identity was located. They would turn to it while eschewing the ideologies of their education. For them, the folk sensibility was the closest thing to an indigenous Jamaicanness. But the divide remained and the imposition of the educated middle class imagination on the philosophies of the working class highlighted how wide it was. The middle-class writer was constantly embracing the role of the medium – the one called to give voice to the voiceless. A noble pursuit, no doubt, but one that resulted in a strangely bastardised set of ideologies and contradictory perceptions of self that sent writers scurrying to *The Tempest* for some poetic rationalisation of a dilemma that manifested itself in questions of language, religion, race and politics.

Tellingly, very few writers, during the spate of West Indian literature in the fifties and early sixties, dealt with middle-class themes. The exceptions were important in Jamaican writing for their honesty: John Hearne, who was constantly preoccupied with the brown Jamaican and who struggled with issues of representation in his work, and Neville Dawes, whose work was marked by the depiction of the character's journey from peasant poverty to middle class alienation.

The problem was that many of the writers who wanted to speak on behalf of the folk were in fact pretenders to the title Caliban. They had learned too well Prospero's wishes and only half-heartedly protested when they were asked to use his language. Their affinity was more to Ariel. Caliban was elsewhere formulating his own unorthodox rebellion. If Shakespeare's Caliban had to fail – for Shakespeare understood that Caliban would never truly capitulate, would never learn to play Prospero's game – Caliban, in the context of Caribbean society, was busy creating his own masque, his own play, a sideshow for Shakespeare, but a full-blown drama for and about himself.

There were those searching for Caliban. Kamau Brathwaite in his search settled on jazz. Caliban was in jazz. But Brathwaite knew he was borrowing, going outside the history of the Caribbean to find a neatly defined aesthetic. It worked, but it was always somewhat strained because Brathwaite's literary theory remained largely removed from the world he sought to explore. It was true that jazz came out of a black, urban environment that was intent on defining its own character and establishing its own parameters of meaning. In the work of Brathwaite and Tony McNeill it made for a superb metaphor, but even in America, jazz in 1966 was esoteric, and, in some ways, had become elitist. In the Caribbean jazz was present, but it was a minority interest that did not become a significant part of Jamaican culture until it was absorbed and transformed (along with African-American R & B) as one of the elements in Ska. It is not surprising that in the 60s and 70s there were few writers in the Caribbean who would regard themselves as jazz novelists or poets.

Reggae's emergence has changed much of that dilemma of seeking to find models of poetic construction in the culture of the working class community. Reggae has ensured that the middle class artist no longer feels the burden to speak for the voiceless, for reggae is that missing voice. Reggae, moreover, could not be dismissed as quaintly folkish or subcultural. It has always been a form of expression that embraces contemporary technology, has developed its own business organisations (where by contrast is the Caribbean publishing industry?) and has become a truly international musical form. Above all, it is a music which is heard throughout the society. Reggae is, like Rastafarianism, a Jamaican creation – a thoroughly Jamaican creation and it has, in that sense, a quality of authenticity that is appealing to the writer. Reggae has allowed the middle-class artist to listen and learn from a poetics which has emerged out of working class culture. Reggae provided an aesthetic that crosses cultural, racial and class divides.

The idea for a book of reggae poems is not especially new. In the 1970s, Kamau Brathwaite may have envisaged such a book as he collected new and innovative poetry in his important issues of *Savacou*, some of which contain the first publications of dub poetry and reggae-driven verse. Other anthologies have tried to acknowledge the connection between oral performance and popular culture and the poetry emerging in the Caribbean. *Voice Print*, an anthology edited by Stewart Brown, Mervyn Morris and Gordon Rohlehr seeks to do this by focusing on what they describe as "Oral and Related Poetry from the Caribbean". Paula Burnett's *Penguin Book of Caribbean Verse* is careful to include the lyrics of popular musicians and folk artists as part of the oral influence. But her anthology establishes a divide and sticks carefully to it: a divide between the oral and the scribal. Indeed, few anthologies from the Caribbean ignore the relationship between the oral and the written. All contain dub poems, and other oral pieces along with the more conventional poetic forms. What *Wheel* offers, however, is a more complex thesis. *Wheel* argues that there is such a thing as a reggae aesthetic and that this aesthetic has come to shape the writing of all kinds of poets from all over the world. Selecting reggae allows this book to look at one important aesthetic force and to see how it has given shape to the poetics of writers who work in conventional as well as non-conventional forms. This anthology, then, finds its *raison d'etre* not just in an acknowledgement of the importance of the oral and popular traditions to conventional verse, but in the basic thesis that there is such a thing as a reggae aesthetic and that there exist examples of it in the works of many writers. One would have to look to the way in which the Blues and Jazz traditions have spawned some important anthologies in the United States to see parallels to this book.

Readers may well turn to this anthology expecting a plethora of what is called dub poetry. There is a good selection of dub poems contained here, but this is not a dub poetry collection, if dub poetry is defined as poetic expression that relies primarily on performance and more often than not on a band playing behind the words. But if dub poetry is defined as the poetry that has been shaped and given character by reggae music, then much of what is contained here is dub poetry. Much, but not all, by no means all. What this anthology presumes is a reggae aesthetic – an aesthetic that one can discern in the dub poetry of Linton Kwesi Johnson *and* in the sonnets of Geoffrey Philp. Sometimes these poems do not look anything like a reggae song, but at their core and in their attitudes they represent a dialogue with reggae. In some instances, this dialogue is not one of celebration, but one of deep questioning, as in Anthony McNeill's "Ode to Brother Joe", Mervyn Morris' "Rasta Reggae" and Opal Adisa Palmer's "Ethiopia Under a Jamaican Mango Tree" – all poems questioning the usefulness of the utopian dream of Rastafarianism which is elemental to the reggae song. These are poems of confrontation and dialogue and yet they remain deeply inscribed, in style and form, in the reggae aesthetic. Olive Senior's "Meditation on Yellow" has no obvious reggae allusions, but it is clear that the world that she creates and the woman she has drawn are steeped in the attitudes of a Jamaica long inscribed in the rebellion and defiance of the reggae song. It is in the tone and character of the poem that I discern the reggae sensibility. Reading these poems in the light of a reggae aesthetic shows that the influence of reggae goes beyond the predictable signs that make it easy to identify dub poetry as a reggae verse form. It is important to do this if the true weight and rich complexity of the reggae aesthetic is to be fully grasped.

For many of the poets collected here, reggae is an occasional influence, an alternative aesthetic that generates poems I admire. But these poets would not claim to be reggae poets, largely because there isn't a broad enough definition of a reggae poet to make this label work. Poets like James Berry, Fred D'Aguiar, Stewart Brown and Ramabai Espinet would not call themselves reggae poets, but they would also acknowledge that they have, in many ways, come under the influence of the reggae song and that this has added a dimension to their work. Their poems selected for this anthology reflect a dialogue between the poets' imaginations and the reggae ethos. There are other poets whose entire work can be treated to a largely reggae reading, though the poets themselves may not advocate this focus. Poets such as Rohan Preston, Lorna Goodison, Kendel Hippolyte, Jean Binta Breeze and Dennis Scott have all produced enough work connected with reggae to make a reading of their work in the light of a reggae aesthetic both valid and revealing.

In selecting the poems for this anthology I found far more than I needed or could include and trimmed the selections down to what I felt were representative samples. I am aware that many of the poets included here would have wanted to offer me other poems rooted in the reggae aesthetic that they considered more fitting. I did not approach the poets themselves when making the selections, nor did I put out a general call. Instead I pored through anthology after anthology and collection after published collection to find material because I wanted to show that there was already a body of published work that made the case for the reggae aesthetic. No doubt a follow-up anthology could include more new voices and previously unpublished poems. I did worry that my selection would be entirely Jamaican, but I need not have done so. Barbadian Kamau Brathwaite remains one of the first poets to write in the cadence and ethos of reggae in his work (see "Wings of a Dove" in *The Arrivants*), and the range of non-Jamaican voices demonstrates how reggae has permeated the experience of blacks (and whites) all over the world. There are no doubt some significant omissions where problems over permissions and fees precluded the use of the work of some writers' whom I considered for inclusion.

I went back to the poetry of the seventies to show the first steps in the development of reggae poetry, though the work of Louise Bennett from the 1950s and 60s is clearly an important precursor. At least four poems devoted to the imagination and artistry of Don Drummond are included, although Drummond, strictly speaking, was not a reggae artist. His musical career ended before the emergence of reggae, but his legacy of ska music was influential on the work of many reggae artists in the late sixties and early seventies. Drummond was, too, with his a troubled sufferer persona, the archetype of the prophetic reggae artist. Drummond's influence is acknowledged by a number of the poets including Tony McNeill in his warning poem to Marley, "Bob Marley", and by Norman Weinstein in his surreal sequence of poems about reggae and ska. But in Lorna Goodison's "Don D" and Mervyn Morris's "Valley Prince" Drummond is co-opted into the ethos of reggae, the spirit of the reggae icon. Here the artist represents the voice of the people, the voice of the society, even as the artist is celebrated as an isolated figure – alienated and trying to reconcile the conflicting pulls on his life and his imagination. That these poets see in Drummond the archetype of the Caribbean or Jamaican poet/artist suggests that they have seen in the emergence of the popular artist a model for the position of the artist in the society. They come to the image with a combination of admiration and questioning. This is a dialogue that leads to very important poetry.

At one time I thought of including a selection of lyrics from the songs of such artists as Bob Marley, Winston Rodney and Joseph Hill of Culture. A collection of such lyrics would show beyond all doubt how pertinent, imaginative and poetic the best reggae lyrics have been. In the end I chose not to do this. Marley's lyrics on the page are only a pale simulacrum of their presence in recorded song where they are indivisible from the song's melody, the singer's phrasing and tone of voice. They were never intended to be read separately from performance.

What is consistent about the poems in *Wheel and Come Again* is the way that language is used. Much of the language is nation language and especially that flecked with Rasta-speech and the spirit of Rasta invention. The *I* in Dennis Scott's poems, for instance, is a complex and ambiguous *I*, an *I* that recurs in the poetry of Morris and McNeill and of Afua Cooper. This use of nation language is different from the traditional use of dialect as a way to define character – to create a persona separate from the poet. Now the nation language (in all its registers) *is* the voice of the poem, it is the voice of the narrative and of the ideology of the poet. This is, in significant measure, a product of reggae because particularly in the work of Bob Marley, Lee 'Scratch' Perry and Burning Spear, we hear the complexities of philosophical and social analysis and the dialect of love and sexuality contained in the nation language of Jamaica. There is a confidence in the potential of this language to deal both in profundities *and* in nonsense that owes much to the work of these reggae artists who use the language of their society without either the self-consciousness or the pretence common to some of the efforts at "dialect" poetry in the past.

There are some technical problems involved in publishing written nation language, particularly because there is as yet no accepted standard orthography. Inevitably, spellings vary from poet to poet. I have retained the original published versions because I felt it would be unwise to tinker when there is no accepted standard. The reader should read such words out loud and trust their ears and their sense of context.

Ultimately, though, the reader should be left with a sense of the breadth of language range that operates in the Caribbean, a range that is dynamic and filled with surprises, the kind of surprises and puns and other word games that make for powerful and engaging poetry. I hope the reader will come to this collection with the same sense of anticipation and expectation of the known and unknown, the familiar and the new as they would going to a reggae concert, a reggae dance in some over-heated basement in the middle of a first world winter, or slipping a new reggae CD into the digital guts of a CD player. There is a sensuality to much of this poetry that is engrossing. There is a profound quality of social consciousness and responsibility cooling in these lines. Each voice is searching for a way to fire the conventions of poetry with the spirit and force of reggae. This volume, then, points to a new approach to Caribbean poetry, an approach that accepts that a distinctive aesthetic has now emerged and is giving shape to the writing. Just as the position of Blues in African-American writing has forced critics to develop a whole new series of tools and considerations to evaluate that work, so this anthology indicates the necessity of such an approach to recent Caribbean writing.

But *Wheel* is no academic treatise – it is an attempt to hold a dancehall session in poetry, to take readers to the heart of reggae and carry them into the compelling seduction of the drum and bass. If this collection can manage this, then it will have done precisely what I hoped it would when I embarked on this project.

But it may all be in vain, this attempt to render the spirit of reggae music into the different music of words placed one after the other. After all, reggae is never just the words alone, the text alone; there are other elements that go beyond the simple logic of meaning. There is something beyond empirical theory in the pulse of the bass as a heart beat, or the pattern and tone of the singing as a capturing of the memory of West African musicality to explain that strange something that makes a reggae sound, properly rendered, a moment of sheer grace. The poet cannot hope to recreate this magical pull of sound and memory that is called "the groove", the "rightness and tightness" of music at its most passionate and intelligent. Perhaps what these poems reveal is that there is something else, equally but differently magical, that can occur in the poem. What is common to both the truly outstanding dub poets and the best of the poets who approach reggae from a more conventional direction is a force of imagination, a capacity to convey this in exact and striking verbal forms and a technical inventiveness in handling poetry's own musicality of sound.

It was a three-way call late one night in 1996. In Chicago, poet Rohan Preston was glorying in a child to come; in New York, Colin Channer was celebrating a good book deal with Random House; and I was in South Carolina beaming as this gathering of American-based Jamaican voices tried to speak the importance of reggae in their writing. It was during that conversation that Channer coined the term "Natural Mysticism" for what this reggae aesthetic was about. Immediately, we began to justify this fitting label, its appropriateness, not unaware of its catchy connections with another revolutionary idea of loftier vintage: Magic Realism. The idea fed a wave of activity in me that would, within a year, culminate in this anthology of reggae poems; a book about the reggae aesthetic (*Natural Mysticism: Towards A New Reggae Aesthetic in*

Caribbean Writing), and a collection of new reggae-based poems (*Shook Foil*). Channer would complete his own reggae-flecked novel *Waiting in Vain,* in that time, while Preston would complete several cycles of poems rooted in that aesthetic. This was a fruitful and affirming conversation that admittedly deteriorated into vainglorious intimations of grandeur: the world-transforming new order: the Second Coming buoyed by Reggae's Mystique, Nobel Prizes, Pulitzers, Whitbreads, Bookers. It was getting late and somebody's phone bill was going to be immense. The conversation ended with appropriate quotations from some non-sense reggae lyrics, but the process of forging a sense of poetic identity was well in place.

The nature of the reggae aesthetic in literary practice will change, as reggae too will continue to evolve, but there is an important moment in the development of Caribbean literature here. I feel quite assured in stating and in celebrating this.

JOHN AGARD

FOR BOB MARLEY

Dreadlocks gone
from I an I crown of glory
and what to be got to be

yet nobody believe Marley dying
no woman no cry crying
out from the sound system of a heart
Who Jah bless no man curse
bu' the cancer getting worse

cutting off of locks
a necessary condition
for treating the tumour of the brain
Him lion mane shorn like a lamb
Him born again
walking through the valley of the shadow of

pain

yet nobody believe Marley dying
nobody believe the reggae rainbow
flying home to Zion
without him dreadlocked halo

We all know
Babylon is one
to cut off Rasta hair
and throw Rasta in prison

But this time doctor say
for treatment to work
dreadlocks must go
Strange the ways of Babylon
stranger still the ways of Jah

yet nobody believe Marley dying
dying of cancer in Miami

He who touch no pork
no junk food whether in London or New York
believed only in the natural
I-tal vital
ate of fresh herbs of the field
as laid down by the Good Book
on tours always taking his own cook
He left bodyguards to politicians
touching no nicotine
partaking only of the holy weed
which the press
say was taken to excess
but which Marley I'm sure
would say is the key to the inner door
the holy herb
filling his mind with the holy word
and the flight of doves
at peace in the shadow of Solomon
Got to have kaya

Strange the ways of Babylon
Now herbless and lockless
this child of Jah in the wilderness
of a malignant growth
yet nobody believe Marley dying
dying of cancer in Miami
it can't be it can't be

shout it out from Trenchtown to Zimbabwe
shake the cornerstone of the Cedars of Lebanon
it can't be   no   not Marley

But in the grounation of a mother grief
one woman hold her head and cry
one woman Cedella Booker mother of Bob
hear her earthwise heart whisper
one bright morning when my work is over
and deep down she know the time come
cause Jah giveth and Jah taketh
and holding her son locksless head
she reads his favourite psalm
to help him home

     'The Lord is my shepherd; I shall not want.
     He maketh me to lie down in green pastures
     He leadeth me beside the still waters...'

And from the logwood burning love
of her womanheart
black womanhurt inward yearning
Rita Marley I-rie queen
watches the fiery red gold and green
drifting to galaxies
beyond West Kingston
Fly away home to Zion

but thoughts of distant planets
don't make her forget
the sound of bullets
the violence in the streets
the attempts on Marley life
by shootdown hit-and-run
Trenchtown thug politics

and caressing the star of his head
she misses them locks
natty dread natty dread
that often touched her as they lay loving
and to herself she make a vow
not to send her Bob
locksless to his Zion

to the shorn lamb
she shall return him lion mane
she shall see that in his casket
his face is draped
with rays of sun
him antennae of salvation
picking up positive vibration
in his casket
I and I crown of locks
the Bible in one hand
his guitar in the other
like gifts from an ancient Egyptian queen
sending her loved one home to Ra
sending her loved one home to Jah

    Everything going to be allright
    everything going to be allright
    no woman no cry
    Marley don't need death
    to make a exodus to history
    Marley don't need politician
    to deem him honourable
    Marley would hate a tearful elegy

    so let this poem be a spliff
    and from the heart of Harlem let a riff
    of tribute curl skyward
    Let Stevie Wonder in his rainbow darkness

masterblast your song of praise
to the secret ears of plants
from the ground of Zimbabwe
let freedom song resound
and see the children dance
O see the children dance
forget your sorrow and dance
Let the nyabingi drums chant
a celebration of positive vibration
Let Cedella take a gospel song
and with a mother tender care
nurse it to a breath of reggae
Let the I-threes incense the sky
with riddims of blessings
Little darling please don't shed no tears
and see the children dance
O see the children dance
forget your trouble and dance

cause today is a day beyond mourning
today the sun is a mane of flame
raining a plea to mankind

    one love
    one heart

Listen those of you who have ears to hear
Listen those of you who have ears to hear.

LILLIAN ALLEN

RIDDIM AN' HARDTIMES

An' him chucks on some riddim
    an' yu hear him say
        riddim an' hardtimes
          riddim an' hardtimes

music a prance
dance inna head
drumbeat a roll
hot like lead

Mojah Rasta gone dread
natt up natt up
irie
red

riddim a pounce wid a purpose
Truths and Rights
mek mi hear yu

drum
drum drum
drumbeat
heart beat
pulse beat
drum

roots wid a Reggae resistance
riddim
noh Dub them call it
riddim an' hardtimes

dem pounce out the music
carv out the sounds

hard hard
hard like lead
an it bus im in im belly
an' a Albert Johnson
Albert Johnson dead
dead
dead

but this ya country hard eh?
ah wey wi come ya fa?
wi come ya fi better
dread times
Jah signs

drum beat drum beat
pulse beat
heart beat
riddim an' hardtimes
riddim an' hardtimes

riddim an' hard
                hard
                hard

RUBBA DUB STYLE INNA REGENT PARK

Monday morning broke
news of a robbery
Pam mind went
couldn't hold the load
dem took her to the station
a paddy wagon
screaming...
her Johnny got a gun
from an ex-policeman

Oh Lawd, Oh Lawd Oh Lawd eh ya
a wey dis ya society a do
to wi sons

Rub a dub style
inna Regent Park
mon a dub it inna dance
inna Regent Park
oh lawd oh lawd

"forget yu troubles and dance"
forget yu bills them
an irie up yuself
forget yu dreams gathering dusts
on the shelves
dj rapper hear im chant
pumps a musical track
for im platform
cut it wild
sey de system vile
dubbing it inna dance
frustration pile
a different style
inna regent park

could have been a gun
but's a mike in his hand
could've been a gun spilling out the lines
but is a mike
        is a mike
                is a mike
Oh Lawd Oh Lawd Oh Lawd

riddim line vessel im ache
from im heart outside
culture carry im past
an steady im mind
man tek a draw an feeling time

words cut harsh   try to find
explanations
de sufferings of de times

"forget yuh troubles and dance"
forget yu bills dem
an irie up yu self
forget yu dreams gatherin
dust   dust   dust

is a long time wi sweating here
is a long time wi waiting here
to join society's rites
is a long time wi beating down yu door

is a long time since we mek the trip
cross the Atlantic
on the slave shippppppp
is a long time wi knocking
an every time yu slam the door
sey: no job
discrimination injustice
a feel the whip lick
an is the same boat
        the same boat
            the same boat
Oh Lawd   Oh Lawd   Oh Lawd   eh ya

dj chant out cutting it wild
sey one hav fi dub it inna different style
when doors close down on society's rites
windows will prey open
in the middle of the night
dashed hopes run wild
in the middle of the night
Oh Lawd   Oh Lawd   Oh Lawd   eh ya

EDWARD BAUGH

NIGGER SWEAT

'Please have your passport and all documents out
and ready for your interview. Kindly keep them dry.'
(Notice in the waiting-room of the US Embassy, Visa Section,
Kingston, Jamaica, 1982.)

No disrespect, mi boss,
just honest nigger sweat;
well almost, for is true
some of we trying to fool you
so we can lose weself
on the Big R ranch
to find a little life,
but boss, is hard times
make it, and not because
black people born wutliss:
so, boss, excuse this nigger sweat.
And I know that you know it
as good as me,
this river running through history,
this historical fact, this sweat
that put the aroma
in your choice Virginia
that sweeten the cane
and make the cotton shine;
and sometimes I dream a nightmare dream
that the river rising, rising
and swelling the sea and I see
you choking and drowning
in a sea of black man sweat
and I wake up shaking
with shame and remorse

for my mother did teach me,
Child, don't study revenge.
Don't think we not grateful, boss
how you cool down the place for we comfort,
but the line shuffle forward
one step at a time
like Big Fraid hold we,
and the cool-cut, crew-cut Marine boy
wid him ice-blue eye and him walkie-talkie
diss walk through the place and pretend
him no see we.
But a bring me handkerchief,
mi mother did bring me up right,
and, God willing, I keeping things cool
till we meet face to face,
and I promise you, boss,
if I get through I gone,
gone from this bruk-spirit, kiss-me-arse place.

JAMES BERRY

SOUNDS OF A DREAMER
(Remembering Bob Marley)

1st VOICE:
Two-blood passion man,
come walk on.
Come walk on and make the scene
with usual incantatory spell.
Come word-out a continued cry.
Word out hell hauntings all *sweet sweet*
Make bad-man history get a trial.
Make rhythms echo death of pain,
music tickle feet,
load fall away.
Come, man. Come walk on and make the scene.

2nd VOICE
Out on a limb, a cooing dove:
could we love and be loved?
Could we touch I and I to find
wonders of eye to eye confined
in a wash of redemption song.

1st VOICE
        O you spinner of storm into song
        like instrument of steel pan!

Well well distressed
he met the losers poverty dressed.
Met them telling him:
all through every night long
all through every day long
living stops the same –
Bad-Dice Man beats them at the game.

2nd VOICE
Hungrybelly and Fullbelly dohn walk same track.
And Hope was born affected.
She was born crippled.
And *such such* a good looker.
Such fine dresser and responsive singer.

Hears music, hears paradise:
everything, everything, in her eyes.
Sings, you hear a reggae queen.
Loved by all each time seen.
Now just a haunting
of love that stresses hunger,
of love that stresses hunger.

But beaten down fire what a-smoulder
brings out yard of brothers and sisters
to a hymnal of the flaming reggae
in the music of roots what deh yah
a-keep the temple open for Jah.

1st VOICE
        O you voice of sun-sounds
        in peace-and-love globe rounds!

Well well distressed
he met the losers poverty dressed.
Met them telling him:
ways of an eternal job
keep up other sides wrong sides,
Making a good chance a game unfair.
Bad-Dice Man throws bad dice,
Bad dice, dice loaded. Loaded.

2nd VOICE
Hungrybelly and Fullbelly dohn walk same track
And the dream was affected.
She was born crippled,

yet helped his lyrics, and moves
that urged his peace and love
where too many two-sides are wrong sides.

But beaten down fire what a-smoulder
brings out yard of brothers and sisters
for the come in of calm time
in the come in of the holy wine
bringing in the hidden for discovery.

1st VOICE
     O you fanfare echoing dayclean —
     fresh echoes we ride on!

Well well distressed
he met the losers poverty dressed.
Met them telling him:
all through every night long
all through every day long
we the losers the generations left,
we still stand out here bereft.
Bad-Dice Man throws bad dice,
bad dice, dice loaded. Loaded.

2nd VOICE
Trees a-blossom
but too much young fruits fall
like it was custom.
Trees a-blossom
but too much young fruits fall
like it was a custom.
And the exodus, exodus, exodus
is O such a silent exodus!

All of you famine skeletons,
all of you moneyless daughters and sons,
say: brother dohn cry.
Say: sister, dohn cry.

We are recollecting to collect back,
a-try for pace and space unplaced
for free rightness of a future,
for free rightness of a future.
The sea does not divide for us to cross
we have to swim and cut our path
And everything's gonna be all right.

1ST VOICE
O, remember –
he walked town streets, all trendy
looking for a scene-change that's friendly
together head to head with Jah
a-confirm rights of person to person law.
Remember – sounds in the yard
from country horns and strings he heard
in the evening cleared of storm
when friends roasted up *fresh fresh* corn
and they walked in the love of others,
love recharging survivors,
in a little time
that was only such a little time.

2ND VOICE
Wild love stands to devour;
tamed love will lend and borrow.
Losers survive with songs of stress;
winners live with excess.

Could we love and be loved
forever loving Jah
saying, say:
forever loving Jah,
forever loving Jah?

1ST VOICE
        O – you new bridge we use now
        with a garland of gold on show!

MARION BETHEL

REGGAE PROPHECY

Heavy reggae beat thumps
heart murmurs wail foreseen
pain, lips, fingers tune up
to a simple melody harmoni-
zing with a moaning gusty
bass skin-dew signals the
dawn of a new coupling song
hips thighs ska rocksteady
reggae morning breezes of
summer heat makes the rhythms
one. Tongue-whipped instru-
ments screaming their last
refrain, love sweated bodies
cling to the last, plaintive
note sucked into oblivion.
Every beat has its measured
end leaving echoes resonant
relentless of a future song.

KAMAU BRATHWAITE

STONE

**for
Mikey Smith
stoned to death on Stony Hill, 1954–1983**

When the stone fall that morning out of the johncrow sky
it was not dark at first · that opening on to the red sea humming
but something in my mouth like feathers · blue like bubbles
carrying signals & planets & the sliding curve of the world like a water pic
ture in a raindrop when the pressure · drop

When the stone fall that morning out of the johncrow sky
i couldn't cry out because my mouth was full of beast & plunder
as if i was gnashing badwords among tombstones
as if that road up stony hill · round the bend by the church

yard · on the way to the post office · was a bad bad dream
& the dream was like a snarl of broken copper wire zig zagg.
ing its electric flashes up the hill & splitt· ing spark & flow.
ers high· er up the hill · past the white houses & the ogogs bark.
ing all teeth & fur· nace & my mother like she up · like she up · like she up

side down up a tree like she was scream· like she was scream· ing no & no
body i could hear could hear a word i say · ing · even though
there were so many poems left & the tape was switched on & runn· ing &
runn· ing & the green light was red & they was standin up there & ever· where
in london & amersterdam & at unesco in paris & in west berlin & clapp·ing &

clapp· ing & clapp· ing & not a soul on stony hill to even say amen
& yet it was happening happening happening · the fences begin
to crack in i skull · & there was loud bodoooooooooooooooooooogs like
guns goin off · them ole time magnums · or like a fireworks a dreadlocks
was on fire · & the gaps where the river comin down & the drei gully

where my teeth use to be smilin · & i tuff gong tongue
that use to press against them & parade pronunciation ·now unannounce
& like a black wick in i head & dead · &
it was like a heavy heavy riddim low down in i belly · bleedin dub · &
there was like this heavy heavy black dog thump· in in i chest & pump·ing

murdererrrrrrrrrrrrrrrrrrrrrrrrrrrrrrrrrrrrrrrrrrrrrrrrrrrrrrrrrrrrrrrrrrrr

& i throat like dem tie· like dem tie · like dem tie a tight tie around
it · twist· ing my name quick crick · quick crick · & a never wear neck
tie yet · & a hear when de big boot kick down i door · stump
in it foot pun a knot in de floor· board · a window slam shut at de back
a mi heart · de itch & ooze & damp a de yard in my silver tam·

bourines closer & closer · st joseph marching bands crash· ing &
closer &

bom si· cai si· cai si· ca boom ship bell ·bom si· ca boom ship bell

& a laughin more blood &
spittin out

lawwwwwwwwwwwwwwwwwwwwwwwwwwwwwwwwwwwwwwwwd

& i two eye lock to the sun & the two sun starin back black from de grass
& i bline to de butterfly fly

in

·

& it was like a wave on stony hill caught in a crust of sun
light

·

& it was like a matchstick schooner into harbour
muffled in the silence of it wound

.

& it was like the blue of speace was filling up the heavens with it thunder
& it was like the wind was grow· ing skin

the skin had hard hairs · hardering

.

it was like marcus garvey rising from his coin · stepping towards his people
crying dark

& every mighty trod he word· the ground fall dark & hole be·
hine him like it was a bloom ex·. ploding sound · my ears was bleed·

ing sound

.

& i was quiet now because i had become that sound
the sun· light morning washed the coral limestone harsh

against the soft volcanic ash· i was
& it was slipping past me into water & it was slipping past me into
root· i was

& it was
slipping past me into flower & it was
ripping upwards into shoot· i was

& every politrician tongue in town was lash
ing me with spit & cut· rass wit & ivy whip & wrinkle jumbimum
it was like warthog · grunt · ing in the ground

& children running down the hill run right on through the splash
of pouis that my breathe· ing made when it was howl & red & bubble
& sparrow twits pluck tic & tap· worm from the grass

as if i man did have no face · as if i man did never in this place

.

When the stone fall that morning out of the johncrow sky
i could not hold it brack or black it back or block it off or limp
away or roll it from me into memory or light or rock it steady into night be

cause it builds me now with leaf & spiderweb & soft and crunch & like the
powderwhite & slip & grit inside your leather· boot & fills my blood
with deaf my bone with hobble· dumb & echo· less neglect neglect neglect neglect

&
lawwwwwwwwwwwwwwwwwwwwwwwwwwwwwwwwwwwwwwwwwd

.

i am the stone that kills me

JEAN BINTA BREEZE

RIDDYM RAVINGS
(The Mad Woman's Poem)

de fus time dem kar me go a Bellevue
was fi di dactar an de lanlord operate
an tek de radio outa mi head
troo dem seize de bed
weh did a gi mi cancer
an mek mi talk to nobady
ah di same night wen dem trow mi out fi no pay de rent
mi haffi sleep outa door wid de Channel One riddym box
an de DJ fly up eena mi head
mi hear im play seh

Eh, Eh,
no feel no way
town is a place dat ah really kean stay
dem kudda — ribbit mi han
eh — ribbit mi toe
mi waan go a country go look mango

fah wen hungry mek King St pavement
bubble an dally in front a mi yeye
an mi foot start wanda falla fly
to de garbage pan eena de chinaman backlat
dem nearly chap aff me han eena de butcha shap
fi de piece a ratten poke
ah de same time de mawga gal in front a mi
drap de laas piece a ripe banana
a mi — ben dung — pick i up — an nyam i
a dat time dem grab mi an kar mi back a Bellevue
dis time de dactar an de lanlord operate
an tek de radio plug outa mi head
den sen mi out, seh mi alright
but — as ah ketch back outa street

ah push een back de plug
an ah hear mi DJ still a play, seh

Eh, Eh,
no feel no way
town is a place dat ah really kean stay
dem kudda — ribbit mi han
eh — ribbit mi toe
mi waan go a country go look mango

Ha Haah... Haa

wen mi fus come a town
mi use to tell everybady 'mawnin'
but as de likkle rosiness gawn outa mi face
nobady nah ansa mi
silence tun rags roun mi bady
in de mids a all de dead people dem
a bawl bout de caast of livin
an a ongle one ting tap mi fram go stark raving mad
a wen mi siddung eena Parade
a tear up newspaper fi talk to
sometime dem roll up
an tun eena one a Uncle But sweet saaf
yellow heart breadfruit
wid piece a roas saalfish side a i
an if likkle rain jus fall
mi get cocanat rundung fi eat i wid
same place side a weh de country bus dem pull out
an sometime mi a try board de bus
an de canductar bwoy a halla out seh
'dutty gal, kum affa de bus'
ah troo im no hear de riddym eena mi head
same as de tape weh de bus driva a play, seh

Eh, Eh,
no feel no way
town is a place dat ah really kean stay

dem kudda — ribbit mi han
eh — ribbit mi toe
mi waan go a country go look mango
so country bus, ah beg yuh
tek mi home
to de place, where I belang...

an di dutty bway jus run mi aff

Well, dis mawnin, mi start out pon Spanish Town Road
fah mi deh go walk go home a country
fah my granny use to tell mi how she walk fram wes
come a town
come sell food
an mi waan ketch home befo dem put de price pon i,
but mi kean go home dutty?
Fah mi parents dem did sen mi out clean
Ah!
See wan stanpipe deh!
So mi strip aff all de crocus bag dem
an scrub unda mi armpit
fah mi hear de two mawga gal dem laas nite
a laugh an seh
who kudda breed smaddy like me?
A troo dem no know seh a pure nice man
weh drive car an have gun
visit my piazza all dem four o'clock a mawnin
no de likkle dutty bwoy dem weh mi see dem a go home
wid
but as mi feel de clear water pon mi bady
no grab dem grab mi
an is back eena Bellevue dem kar mi
seh mi mad an bade naked a street
well dis time de dactar an de lanlord operate
an dem tek de whole radio fram outa mi head
but wen dem tink seh mi unda chloroform
dem put i dung careless

an wen dem gawn
mi tek de radio
an mi push i up eena mi belly
fi keep de baby company
fah even if mi nuh mek i
me waan my baby know dis yah riddym yah
fram before she bawn
hear de DJ a play, seh

Eh, Eh,
no feel no way
town is a place dat ah really kean stay
dem kudda — ribbit mi han
eh — ribbit mi toe
mi waan go a country go look mango

an same time
de dactar an de lanlord
trigger de electric shack
an mi hear de DJ vice bawl out, seh

Murther
Pull up Missa Operator!

EENA MI CORNER

a skengeh
a skengeh
a skengeh pon some chords
eena mi corner
a skengeh pon some chords
eena mi corner
wen boops!
up pap a likkle horner
eena mi furdes corner
jus a
jus a

jus a stretch mi diaphragm
breed een
breed out
breedin easy
jus wen
jus wen
mi a leggo mi laas craas
im jus a
im jus a
a eh i oh oooh
im way troo
de mos complex part
a mi lunar system
dat all wen mi know
im move awn
gawn tune een pon a nex station
mi radio
still ah
still ah
still ah crackle
so mi haffi
mi haffi
mi haffi jus
checka
checka
checka iya iya ites iyah
an jus
flip a switch
tun mi receiva
to transmitta
checkin anadda one
wanderin troo
de sonic boom of a bassline
but wen mi see seh
dis one a forward
pon de same riddym station
breed een
breed out

mi memba
how easy
cho
mi haffi
mi haffi
mi haffi jus

check out

now me one
me jus a
skengeh
skengeh
me jus a
skengeh
pon some chords
eena mi corner

DUBBED OUT

i
search
for words

moving
in their music

not

broken
        by

the
beat

STEWART BROWN

LET THEM CALL IT JAZZ
(for Cedric Brooks)

"Peoples of the Americas
Peoples of the Caribbean
Of Asia and India
Of Africa
WE MUST UNITE!"

The band blares and beats its wrath
to a handful of hypes, mostly whites
whose kulture does not swing
to such sleazy, threatening blues.

But Dr. B and his bad-time band
are already on the road
to Mozambique, are possessed now
by the spirit – and too besides

The institute have paid them
for this Musical Communion
and they **will** blow it, no matter
if they end up on the streets.

WE MUST UNITE!

Tambu man is jungle dyed.
He stared hard at the sun
on that black passage
and now the Niger's flood
still courses/curses in his veins...

It is the tap
       tap root of his fear
       of his fear
       that he fight fight
       fights

"we must unite!"

So he remembers. Hates.
Remembers. Hates.
Remembers. Tries to love. Hates.
He is killing us with iron digits,
gun, gun, Ogun...

WE MUST UNITE!

Basey wows em all, God-damn-it,
with his pearl-bright minstrel grin,
but beneath that smart tuxedo
is a scar-backed leather skin.

The ladies luuuuv his steady rhythms
his firm and impeccable pace,
watch him jive that sweet fat chicken
hear him slap her pretty face.

WE MUST UNITE!

A cat that has stolen the cream
pads across the keyboard. Scat!
But he is in the soul of the pianist
in his seed, this mellow pussycat.

WE MUST UNITE

Don D Junior
has a lot to live
down.
          Indifferent
eyes circle the room
till he blues us, slews
us,
          chews us down
the flower of his
bone.

          He shows us
black horizons,
albino lies,
          terminal greys
of corrosion.

WE MUST UNITE

They broke his wrists when he was young
for stealing cane.
Since then he's tasted paler fruit
and beats the pain
out through his snare. The golden sizzle
is his symbol, he would
break it, smash it, hear it scream.
He is playing them back...
          paying them black.

WE MUST UNITE

The lady smiles,
          wipes herself
                    and slinks out
                              of the alley.

The guitarist
        is so much
                much older
                        than the rest:

remembers
        ragtime and
                harmony,
                        came slowly

to terms with
        the ampli-
                fier, now
                        holidays

in Hawaii.
        They all talk,
                and re-tune,
                        through his solo.

WE MUST UNITE

Someone back there
raped his daughters
fired his village
smashed his gods
and dragged him in chains
to this whip of islands
that he might know his place...

So he forgot.

Now nomad echoes haunt
his trumpet's whine.
He has stared at endless sky,
at the mocking sea

and blows, blows salt shards
of memory till his
bones creak like a corsair's
rigging and his
theme is a vulture gusting
in the Harmattan's
dread cool. He dreams of sand
and the Taureg' s
certainty, he blows, blows
blows his flabby
city arse out of the window,
he remembers...

he has come home...

WE MUST UNITE

A *sufferer* who sneaked in drunk
and for free is moved by the blood

swell, by the race memory
that is his dance... he performs

in his boots and sets fire to his hair:
is hero, warrior, patriarch

to a tiny, terrified, Prince...

WE MUST UNITE

His back aches from too much unpaid labour;
this genteel Rasta with a saxophone lip
is airborne, has beaten gravity.

In Mozambique he killed a cow
and blows now a listless, withering lament
as the brothers stamp across the stage,

they are almost out in Harlem, Sharpville,
Brixton, in Free Town, Addis, Zimbabwe,
in Trench Town, Wait a Bit and Morant Bay...

This musical Mais, the leader of the pack,
has his army massing the foothills
and the squares: come, come, come, come...

we must unite
We Must Unite
WE MUST UNITE

AFUA COOPER

STEPPING TO DA MUSE/SIC
(For Bob Marley)

Bob
You make me move in an ancient way
in an ancient way that my feet never forgot
You make my feet, my body
do things I never thought was possible
You make me do old world dance
Dahomey dance
You make me the priestess
in a pure and sacred way
'we don't need more sorrow'
and my body moves slowly, my arms uplifted
I am offering sacrifice to my ancient God

FRED D'AGUIAR

DREAD

I saw these waves
roping off into strands
that combine to make a fat rope
breaking on mud banks and turning pebbles.

But the strands formed ropes of their own
and before I could name what they were
the ingenius head to which they were plaited
reared up from the tide, widening rings
that marked new heights on the South Bank.

Marley's unmistakable smile
shone through the wash released over his face
by the matted locks. He shook them free
and it was like the Crystal Palace Bowl all over again:
Bob under the lights, when, between chanting down babylon
he rattled his dread and in shaking them a tremor
ran up and down the city knocking points off
the stocks and shares at the Exchange
and noughts off some dealers profits.

He spoke through that smile at me.
"I an' I don't need anyone to speak for I.
Though you see dust where there was a tongue
I man still loud and clear on platinum.
Check your history and you will see
throughout it some other body speak for we;
and when they talk they sounding wise and pure

but when you check it all they spouting is sheer lies.
Look in the river it's a crystal ball;
shout about the pain but don't shut out the bacchanal."

Right then Marley start to skank
his big steps threatened to make the water
breach its banks, Barrier or no Barrier,
this was the dance of the warrior.
The more he stamped the lower in the water he sank
until his dreadlocks returned to the waves I mistook
for plaits doing and undoing themselves.

from GDR
(for Wolfgang Binder)

8   *Now the Two Are One*

Stepback, stepforward; it was that kind of rhythm;
stepback, stepforward, to reggae beat.
Stepback, stepforward and no one to stop you;
stepback, stepforward, so I could go on.

Like he went on, on the roomy dance floor
to bassline and call of the DJ toasting
to the bassline and me thinking, join him, and then not.

DREADTALK
'Cow neva know de use a him tail till fly tek it.'

Who eye pass who eye
who badder dan who
who get juck who carry
blade nah fe get juck
an who lick jackass
get lix like peas
wen ass tun com roun

We all want daughta
fe fadder we chile
but daughta nah want
always absent fadder
or sweet man wid no fucha
wid no ninetofive
nor yard a credit card

An we all want custom car
fe bun-up a bit a bichemin
com sataday nite
instead a midnite pitcha
fe feed we dream wid air
is hot air we desire hot air
for de only car we drive is Tonka

And de only house we gon build
is lego de adverts no it
dem nah see we muchless talk
to we an if yu see a black
face yu see de tail end
a trend or som safety valve
move fe check anadda uprisin

So chase dem educashon
an it tun pan yu an before
yu no it yu get prosessed
brite as dem peas in a can
de britess green dat mek
yu tun-up yu nose at de
real ting it so dull

An it cawn really com
outta pod it muss be spaghetti
dem can mek yu beleave grow
pan tree or money plentiful
to be bandeed aroun wortless
dan de energy it tek fe eat
lettuce leaf an so dem tink

De folds a we brain is cabbage
pan legs only good fo runnin
roun track like jackass or dancin
pan de spat till we drap
yu cawn show me a black
who get to de tap or who nah tek
culcha pan a plate or slate

Anadda new category 'black-british'
a progeny alang a line we battle
thru a gauntlet we a run
an we tekin it up evry time
like we a see carrot but no
stick like we foget de whip
we flick a lick back a brodda

An sista who nah want pickney
she cawn feed juss fe bolsta
brodda ego she nah want revolushonary
role he a hann she so dem a cuss

wan anadda an de table dem a get roun
is a lang way aff if eva an dem
only meet in a posse wid a soun

Far is rave dem want fe rave
com sataday nite an de blues
dem a keep at arms length is de bady
dem a rub-up in a heavy dub stile
it safa dan blade an de adda
blue dat a krawl roun in packs
fe pounce pan we in braad daylite

An it betta dan gettin lack-up
in a ward ware yu cawn let aff
steem widout de vial dem a pump
in yu vane dat a beet out
yu brain till yu feel like fish
outta yu debt in a blue
deepa dan eny noshan

An dese days we always pan
haliday at her majesstees
xpense wid noff time fe grow
hare an resentment an vocabulary
fe cuss like caliban wid a girlee
magazine unda we pillow tick enoff
fe muffle we likkle nitely cry

Fe somwan we wooda call crappo
outside or som ringting call freedom
sweet like we seed dat a fall fallow
dat always comin down in seedy
places far de cast a bread
an is cole it cole like snow
hatin it we hate we self

So lay a bet pan de harses
hope fe a brake before yu back
bruk wid overtime enoff fe move
yu miserable backtoback sleep
to de wuk floor cause yu a sweat
like jackass but yu cawn see
de jackey wid blinka pan yu eye

Who gon deny yu yu half
battle a spirit who gon deny
a tirsty mule wata or empty
engin ail wen dem a sit
in de saddle or behine
de wheel cause dem cawn
drive wha nah wuk nar willin

So trow yu head back an droun
yu cares curl-up in a carna
an wet yu pants wake to a wirl
splittin de atom wid evry move
an yu head wish yu self dead
dan dis load yu carry as lang
as yu rememba to noware fe notin

KWAME DAWES

TRICKSTER I
(For Winston Rodney)

Geriatric, wizened, ancient man
with a beard constantly damp

from the flow of good and pleasant
nectar; our cedar of Lebanon,

evergreen griot, since forever chanting
fires down below, blowing up

like volcanoes, revolution;
hearing you now chanting,

isolated prophet on the beaches,
preacher preaching on the burning shore,

yes, Winston Rodney, you could never
forget your roots, such roots,

mellow like waves along the jumping
bassline – this big sound of primordial rhythm.

Yes, if we have a true prophet,
sallow and enigmatic with grandaddy charm,

like John the Baptist with his head full of lichens,
mouth full of locusts and wildest honey;

if ever there was a prophet to walk
these blood-red streets of Kingston,

to sing travelling, travelling, we still travelling –
despite the amassed dead and the fire,

we still travelling–it is you, reggae elderman,
spear flaming through the cankered landscapes:

in the steaming clubs of Halifax,
the kerosene jazz dens of Soweto,

the red-lit drug dens of Amsterdam,
the gritty damp of London's Soho.

We believe in the words of the prophet,
transported as we are by the regal one-drop

to a time when the sea shells glinted
on the splendid Nile, blue and sparkling white.

TRICKSTER II
(For Lee "Scratch" Perry)

1

A voice cried out in the wilderness.
We all came to hear the voice

in the Cockpit valleys, to hear
the man with a skull in his hands.

He was mad.
It was all quite obvious.

We listened but saw no revelations,
just a sweet madness of new rhythms.

Afterwards, we drank mannish water,
ate curried goat, and slept peacefully.

2

Legend puts the Scratch man in trees,
comfortable in this lofty nest, where airwaves

have a clearer path to the sampling antennae
of his dangerous, bright mind.

A few were baptized to the strange
syncopations of unsteady sycophants,

but all looked to see the boy
with a sweet falsetto grained with desert grit

singing the father's songs, just as
the Scratch man prophesied would happen.

3

There would be no wailing songs
without the madness of Scratch Perry;

none of the wild weirdness of *Kaya*,
none of the leap of images, enigmatic

mysteries like scripture; none of the miracle
of guitars twined each on each,

without this man, with his fired
brain and fingers of brilliant innovation

tweaking the nine-track sound board,
teasing out new ways to see heaven.

There would be nothing of the crucifixion,
no resurrection repeated each time another

reggae operator is born, again, again,
no revolution without this locust-eating prophet.

4

All that is left is his bodiless head
chatting, chatting, tongue like a flapping bell,

tongue among the teeth. Salome too is dead,
but the head still creates this twisted

sound here on Switzerland's slopes.
Rastaman defies the chill and prophecies,

his head on a compact disc like a platter
spinning, spinning, spinning, new sounds.

TRICKSTER IV
(For Sister Patra)

Surfing on the dance floor,
balancing that cut of wave,

missing brilliant coral with
a slash and sway of my arm,

watch me fall back, fall back,
then wheel and come again,

something catching me with
invisible hands on the down beat.

Rapid is the chant of the microphone
queen with lyrics like a whip,

lashing me with her rhythm,
then balming me with a sweet

soprano sounding like sticky
on the bubbly bassline.

Sometimes the honey mellows in my soul
and melts my knees to water

and it's a sea surf teasing the sand
back and forth, making froth.

This, this, dis ya sound sweet
you see, sweet like sugar and lime.

Limbo is the way to limber,
seeming to fall back with my arms,

then catch me back with propeller action,
this is the Bogle at work, ya,

on the undulating salt deck of our days
to the sound we lost long ago

when we left the kraal, leaving no forwarding
address, just forwarding to another rock.

But this echo of a land, a land
so far, so far, across the sea,

is lashed to the shock of this lyrical feast,
riding this sweet rhythmic beat.

Somebody say — Vershan! — and then hear
the drum in the sister's tongue,

playing like a gospeller to the wash
of the four-part harmony, dripping sex —

and the way I feel is wild;
wilding up myself with eyes open wide,

surfing on the dance floor
surfing on the dance floor.

And when she's done her lyrical jam
this rest is like old, old, sleep

after sweating sea water, spilling sea water
flowing like that and falling: HEAVY!

SOME TENTATIVE DEFINITIONS I

"Lickle more drums..."
Bob Marley

First the snare crack,
a tight-head snare crack like steel,
rattle, then cut, snap,
crack sharp and ring at the tail;
calling in a mellow mood,
with the bass, a looping lanky
dread, sloping like a lean-to,
defying gravity and still limping

to a natural half-beat riddim,
on this rain-slick avenue.

Sounds come in waves
like giddy party types
bringing their own style and fashion,
their own stout and rum,
their own Irish Moss
to this ram jam session.

Everything get like water now
the way steady hands
curve round a sweat-smooth waistline,
guiding the rub, the dub, so ready.
This sound is Rock Steady
syrup slow melancholy,
the way the guitar tickling
a bedrock drum and bass,
shimmering light over miry clay.

SOME TENTATIVE DEFINITIONS IV
"lick samba, lick samba..."

The girl them a shock out,
preening their garments,
imported from New York,
there on the edge of the crowd.
Everything round on them,
blossoms like bas-relief,
and when they breath,
a still water ripples
circles of undulation.
You will find nothing
to hold onto in their eyes,
transported as they are

by the bashment
sounds. They are waiting
like warm, panting, idle vehicles
before a red light
in sequins and pastels;
everything is riding
from batty to titties,
everything in place
but threatening
a chaos
of unleashed
body parts.
Green.

SOME TENTATIVE DEFINITIONS VII
"...I get to understand yuh been livin' in sin"
Bob Marley, "Bend Down Low"

My fifteen year old
ratchet body
welds itself
to her softer front
and I smell Charlie
mingling with the
chemicals in her hair,
and the rest is a song.

Gyrations of heat,
feet not moving
waistlines going,
trying to find
the groove of sweetest
friction, rolling, rolling,
holding on for dear life
like a buoy on a rocking

sea, like a boat
taken out too far from shore.

In my ears her voice
singing: *Row, fisherman, row*

SOME TENTATIVE DEFINITIONS XI
"Every time I hear the sound of the whip..."
Bob Marley, "Catcha Fire"

For every chekeh of the guitar,
a whip cracks.
How can you hear the sound
and not weep?

Follow the pattern with me,
always on the off.
We are forever searching for spaces
to fill with us.

If you walk straight down on the one,
you will stumble,
cause the reggae walk is a bop
to the off-beat.

We are always finding spaces
in the old scores
to build our homes, temples and dreams,
and we call it back-o-wall.

For every *wooku* of the Hammond B
a body hums.
How can you smell the sound
and still sleep?

BLACK HEART

1

Of the three, one blackheart man lives,
the one whose finger prophesied death
for the Chinese producer, bloodsucker,
pointed to his death, to a heart attack
crashing him down sudden like that,
right there in his office, the crime scene
where hundreds of dreams have been stolen
with a hastily secured signature,
where many voices have been captured
in the cage of black vinyl for a few pounds.
And one normal afternoon, patties consumed,
soft drink gulped quickly, shirt back wet,
after a spate of belching, one vomiting fit,
the man drop dead like that,
lying there like a poem among the carpet
of forty-fives grinning in the fluorescent light.

2

Of the three, one blackheart man lives,
the others are buried beneath the grass,
one the rugged quick tongue of the gangster
dread, stepping razor, crusader of lost causes,
underdog with the wit of a survivor,
his black body boasting bruises
from indiscriminate batons of Babylon's lackeys –
and you can bet he never begged, just cursed
nuff claat, and took the broken jaw
like a trophy – this incarnation
of a Soweto toi toi stumper with no discernible
Boer to make a revolution against,
(for isn't this Paradise where the natives

smile too sweetly to be ruthless?)
just the Shitsem like a windmill.
His eyes would twinkle at the impossible of it
and his mind would construct rastological myths,
the antennae on his head picking up songs
from the waves of the sea at Palisadoes
(and the interviewer nodded with sincere indulgence).
This dread, ambushed by his legacy,
gunned down by an irony so blatant it hurts,
gutted by shot after shot, making him step
searching for solid ground and finding nought
but air, before the head popped. It is finished.

3

Of the three, one blackheart man lives;
the other, the loner, the mystic star-gazer,
the multicoloured coat-wearer, the short explosion,
defied the bullet, but watched
some white man's disease devour his vulnerable
flesh, like treachery, fading, fading
with a whimper against the good night.
The shell could not hold any longer,
crumbled, letting fly his unconquerable soul,
which travelled into mystery and faith;
gone with all the promise,
perhaps because he trusted too much,
perhaps because he embraced too often...

4

Of the three, one blackheart man lives,
the one who will not fly on the iron bird,
not trusting Babylon's contraptions,
sipping, sipping the incense of Jah
and pumping out second-rate dancehall tunes.

A tarnished star, with dubious appeal,
but living through the blackness of a curse,
stoking his own flames of mystery.
He will outlive the poem, he will reorganize
the parts of himself and reinvent his image
before he retires an enigma, a reggae geriatric,
an irrelevant dread with only a satchel
of old songs to his name. Black heart man,
the true duppy conqueror, showing how rude bwoys
grow grey, showing us the sorrowful mortality
of the skanking old man. The others exploded
in the height of their glory, but he will remind us
that all flesh is dust; even the taut drum skin
of the wailing wailer will shrivel too.
It is how it was written, how it has passed
from generation to generation to generation.

RAMABAI ESPINET

MERCHANT OF DEATH

Another Merchant of death
Died in the streets today
And the salt tears
Of mothers caked with grief
Have swelled into his nostrils
To drown and kill him
Twice
And over and over

No merchant's boom
Can bring back to me
My son's sweet smile
As I, now older,
A true night mother
In the City of Dreadful Night
Fail to harness words
To invoke curses

May Kali the destroyer
Breathe her savage prayers
Into your ears
You the merchants of death
So that when, wedded
To the White Lady,
You steal our children
For unabating sacrifice

Our anguished cries
Will pierce and break
Your eardrums

"And if a fire make 'e bun
And if a blood make 'e run"
Our blood wasted for centuries
Will rise and choke, maim and kill
The drifting merchants of death

As, felling from all sides
The beauty of the greening earth
So, small fires burning
Quickened and courageous
Will tear through the brass hammers
The scales, the dust
Coating the tongues and eyes
Of the agents of death

And as you salt yourself
With yellow flags and lucre
All our fallen
Speak through our dumb tongues
And curse
The Merchants of Doom
Watching their first and second
Millions spinning into gold

There is no money
To insulate a merchant of death
From the pure lightning shaft
Of mothers of the night
If you deal death to our young
By our ancestor's strengths
We shall find the way
To the beating heart of death's traders
Not to worry
A smiling dealer tells my boy
Even baboons do: they pray
And they search and find EUPHORIC POISONS

To be human and in pain
Is what they seek
To be weak, errant, susceptible
To escape like you and me

If God is dead
Merchants may have no fear
But neither do I
A grieving mother from
The Kingdom of Ageless Night
The Plain of Imprisoning Day
A place for hidden demons
Of the unwashed human soul

A place of tears
Mothers like me must shed
For our lost children
Lost through coercion
Through overdoses
Through white powder
Through the greed of the enemy
Through inattention

There are no illusions left:
We fight a war
For this green globe
And those whose lovesongs
Have choked backwards
into a dry throat
And whose envy of love
Is ground daily into powder

They are the enemy
My sanity has been dashed
On the rocks below which
My children's brains lie scattered

And grey and whitened
Their thin bones sing of hate
And no leggo — and you —
Death merchant

I have words — bent and riven —
But I have some.
And your absent sensuality
Your empty groomed bodies
Your fitness obsessions
Your karate kid boasts
I will mash to pulp
I will grind to powder

I and I wage war
Trenchtown has never seen
I and I move
With unfettered revenge
Against you
I and I fight
The doomsellers
We claim our children

Now fodder for your use
Their blood cries for justice
For a light and growing world
And for your deeds and more
No curses are loud enough
No mangled flesh — still mourned —
No visions, no sunlight
No beggaries, no love.

LORNA GOODISON

FOR DON DRUMMOND

Dem say him born
with a caul,
a not-quite-opaque
white veil
through which he visioned
only he knew

At birth dem suppose
to bury it
under some special tree.
If we had known
we could have told them
it was to be,
the Angel Trombone Tree.

Taptadaptadaptadada...
Far far East
past Wareika
down by Bournemouth
by the sea,
the Angel Trombone
bell-mouthed sighs
and notes like petals rise
covering all a we.

Not enough notes
to blow back the caul
that descend regularly
and cover this world vision
hiding him from we.

Find a woman
with hair like rivers,
a waist unhinged
and free;
emptied some of the sorrow
from the horn's cup;
into the well below her belly.

She promised to take the caul
from his eyes;
to remove the cold matter
that clouded his eyes;
and stand between him
and
the trombone tree duppy.
The promise dead like history.
Dead like she.

When the caul come again
and covered his eyes:
this time the blade rise
like notes in a scandal
on a street corner
Far far East
past Wareika.

From a Bridge view
the crowd holds notes
One gone...
Don gone...

Lay me down for the band must rest / Yes, Music
        is my occupation
I tired a hold this note / you hold this memory
        For J.F.K., for Me
Mek the slide kotch / is right here so I stop

Belleview is the view I view / Sometime I think
         the whole world mad too.

Behold the house of his feet,
the brown booga
tongue ajar, a door that blow and open and close
         no more.

Fold the dark suit pressed under newspaper,
"Murder" screamed the morning paper,
bring the felt hat
where the caul would hide
to slip down sly and cover his eyes.

And this time do the burial right fi we
Bury the Don under the Angel Trombone Tree.

JAH MUSIC
(For Michael Cooper)

The sound bubbled up
through a cistern one night
and piped its way into
the atmosphere,
and decent people wanted
to know
"What kind of ole nayga music is that
playing on the Government's radio?"
But this red and yellow and dark green
sound,
stained from traveling underground,
smelling of poor people's dinners
from a yard dense as Belgium,
has the healing.
More than weed and white rum healing.

More than bush tea and fever grass cooling
and it pulses without a symphony conductor
all it need is a dub organizer.

HEARTEASE III

In this year of cataclysm pre-predicted
being plagued with dreams
of barefoot men marching
and tall civilizations crumbling
forward to where the gathering, gathering.
Crowdapeople, crowdapeople weep and mourn,
crowdapeople I have seen
packed in Japanese carriers
dark corpses of fallen warriors.
A man wearing a dub image of dirt
roots for fodder in a garbage can
raises a filth-encrusted hand
in a dumb acceptance/greeting
of the stasis on the land.
You see it crowdapeople?

Look and marvel
for I have seen the wonder
of the candyman's posse
women laden like caravels with gold
trimmed in fur, booted in leather
crowned in picture hats
skeeled O Panama.

O wear all this together
in the height of 98-degree weather.
Be acquainted with things to come,
behold the force transparent
mirror that cynical face of the crowd.

Lead them down to the dungeons of darkness
everybody follow.
Soak them in the river of darkness
everybody wallow.

Crowdapeople, crowdapeople.
Big Massa knows
that them powder the devil
and sell you
fi draw im up yu nose.
Crowdapeople,
settle.
Crowdapeople,
level.
When you gone so wide
you will encounter
your true selves again
from the starting-over side.

Then...
Say of the waters of the Hope river
how much sweeter than the ferment wine,
say of the simple leavened loaf
"you are the wafer."
Accept this healing unbeliever
place truth on your tongue deceiver.
Gather, for the days wrongly predicted
by short-tongued ones will end,
these days are but a confused overture to the real
movement, to the pulsing of the rhythms of the
first and last grouping,
we will rise triumphant, clean singing.
For the righteous planted in this place,
have access unlimited to the gardens of grace.
I speak no judgment
this voice is to heal

to speak of possibility
for in dreams Big Massa show me
say,
"I know my people, I created them
their ways are strange only to who will
not love and accept them,
what they do best is to be."
No judgment I speak
that function is not mine
I come only to apply words
to a sore and confused time.

So...
If we mix a solution
from some wild bees' honey
and some search-mi-heart extract
better than red conscience money
and we boil it in a bun-pan
over a sweet wood fire
make the soft smell of healing
melt hard hearts and bare wire.
If we take it and share it
so everyone get a taste
and it reach till
it purge evil from this place
till we start again clean
from the birthplace
of the stream,
while above us arches
the mercy span
a high onyx beam;
reaching from the sea
to the cobalt
blue mountain ridge
the azure forgiving
of the wide mercy bridge.

And...
Suppose we call out the
singers and musicians
by their hidden holy names
and then pull out from the belly
bottom of the drum and the bass
chords that quake evil and
make holy spirit raise,
while the rest of we planting the
undivided, ever-living
healing trees,
what a glory
possibility
soon come
HEARTEASE...

UPON A QUARTER MILLION

Upon a quarter million
With a tape deck of gold
O measure me a mile
of sweet vintage Bob Andy.
Rocking steady
on a pointed principle
Alton Ellis is showing me why
Because he is "Just a guy."
And when I feel it too sweet now
I can't take it no more
The Cables make a connection
from the sky, and ask me "Why,
baby tell me why?"
Sitting beside me
upon this song sentimental journey
is a man with the name "Levi"

written across the front of him creppe.
And I surmise, it must be the name
of his tribe.
And then I think, No, it must be
his rightful name.
For sometimes it would suit a one
to write him name upon himself.
In case Babylon stop you
and fraid claim your tongue
in which case you could just
look down and remind you eye
and say "Yes oppressor
I name is Levi."

Upon a quarter million
with a tape deck of gold
the driver cut a corner
on the bias
and pitch up by the park.
And it come to me
that I must praise all of life
when it light and when it dark.
For all of it is life
and life is all of that
and as I think this so,
I just reach my stop.

KENDEL HIPPOLYTE

REVO LYRIC

sweetchile
dem will say dat
dis eh revolution, stop it
dem go talk about
de People an' de Struggle
an' how in dis dry season
t'ings too dread, too serious
for love

as though
love not a serious t'ing
serious like war, frightenin'
tightenin' de heart strings an'
beatin' a rhythm up a twistin' road
all o' we fraid to dance on

love is a serious t'ing
bringin' you back
to baby-helpless trusting nakedness
whether you want or not
if in truth, in real truth
you love

a serious, serious t'ing:
is walking a high high edge
where looking down or back
would end you
yet forward and up
so dark wid no end

love is – o god sweetheart, dey mus' know!
dey can see!
dis instrument we tryin' to make – society
economics – wood and string

den politics – de major key
but de real, real t'ing
de reason an' de melody
de song we want to sing
is love
is love.

come doudou, sing wid me...

JAH-SON/ANOTHER WAY
(for Jah Howie)
1
who was born, not of a virgin but a real woman
whose father vanished like the holy ghost
who walked the usual crooked mile
out from the high wild mountains of green childhood
down through the mono-crop plantations of the schools
and out into the alleys short-cuts back-streets
side-stepping from the blocks of bank and church
by-passing glass doors glaring windows, watching his reflection
blur into men and manikins arranged inside
dodging the traffic of emotional commerce, the
blaring smiles honking handshakes of the
up-and-coming-at-you 1600 cc. boys.
who ran from three-striped foxes
taxidermised love-birds and sunday citizens
who was jobless, had no fixed abode
who slept in fishing-boats and therefore under stars
whose mind was a tenement-yard of heresies
his head a shaggy thundercloud of darkening questions

his beard glistening with treasons and with ecstasies
who had burned churches blasted government buildings
and grown a garden on their waste —
all in his head
who one day abandoning the highway scramble for the golden fleece
went on to seek the lamb
whose name was Jason till he came to know himself
and then became Jah-Son.

II
but where you going, Jason?
look you mudda crying
your brudda an' sista trying
to get some sense into your head
but dem cyah penetrate; your dread
too thick and knot-up; too much o' tangle
mangle-up question clot-up like bloodstain drying
in your brain — Jason, you go go insane!
Jason, you go dead!

III

there has to be
another way

>   "Too dam' lazy! Ain't he is a carpenter?
>   So why he doh fin' work?"

there has to be

"Oh God Jason, not now!
You cyah just leave me now!"

another way

>   "Come brother, will you give your heart
>   before it is too late?"

has to be

"Comrade, the struggle needs
a thinking man like you."

another way.

IV

Jah sey
Jah Rastafari sey:
see I trod
through valley
see I trod
through town, through stinking alley
see I search
for you
for youth who search
for truth
see I trod
come
I make Man
into God

an' dem a-step outa de shitty
dem vank
lef de school, lef de church, lef de bank
lef de people mek o' concrete and steel
who divide and subtract but cyah feel
de yout' ban that
dem noh wan' that
dem mash it on de ground
as dem step outa de town
outa Sodom and Gomorrah fi go higher!
dem a-shake de city dust offa dem feet
an' a-flash dem natty dread inna de street

dem a-chant an' a-wail an' a-hail bongonyah
Jah-Jah children trod creation on a trail o' bloodfire!

who wan' go
will go
who wan' stay
will stay
whatsover whosoever will

there is a hill called Zion
a sinking ground called Babylon
a so Jah sey

V

a so?
a really, really so?
a two years now Jah-Mighty
an' I still doh know.

here: no cement, no steel
yet something cold
no clock, no wheel
but something
turning wrong and going back.
chaliss burning in my hand, but still
something that i doh hold
something in i know
this not the way

but where to go?

VI

out of the forest, leaving
the twisted track that snaked through bush and coiled round hill
and never led to Zion

turning his back
on blighted gardens, broken earthen-pots
on songs that quavered and then gradually had shrilled to quarrels
on praises that became as thin as smoke
he went down from the psalmist's hill
without hope, not a toke of ganja
nothing to draw on
but himself

VII

down into Mammon's kingdom: among the derelicts the broken the insane
the ones for whom the city's alleyways are made, the back-road
side-street shit-lane people the shanty-minded and the minds like cul-de-sacs,
the shingles of dismantled person the 2 x 4 existences of shaking age with
newsprint peeling off their cracked skins letting in the cold draught of
the cosmos, among the dead-ends of socio-economico-political processes
the snuffed-out butts of a city's nervous smouldering,
Jason among them

has to be

VIII

his life resembled theirs now, driftwood.
cross-currents, ill winds of circumstance
would drag him to a sand-spit of existence
another fool of time who'd lost his substance
and the way home.
he looked on at the dredged and dregged survivors
heard the future like the rumour of a storm
and the present a loud silence.

this?
another cripple at the pool?
and yet how to shout "No!"
to the enormous opening mouth of Nothing?
no way?

no way

IX

he lifted up his eyes, last time –
Zion hill was green and far away.
his gaze dropped to his feet:
barren sidewalk, thin-lipped gutter, asphalt street
and saw grass
and saw how earth itself had shifted, split the sidewalk
how seeds exploding in green flame had caught small fires
all along the cracks and weaknesses of urban surfaces
grass laughing fiercely everywhere once you were looking for it
Zion, shining where it had always been, will always be
NOW, no other time, no other place, NOW
NOW as the grassflesh blazes into singing
splitting the sealed-slab silence of blind city sidewalks
and rustling, passing the word downwind along the pavements
illuminating, witnessing your metamorphosis

Jah-Son.

REGGAE CAT
(For Boston Jack)

                    Something
in the way these alleys twist and
drop into darkness, how they zag
around the corner, jump a ditch,
rub against a zinc fence as they pass
quiet, quiet, avoiding the street-lamps,
telling you ignore the brightness
trust your feet, you won' fall, listen
to the brotherman ahead of you, he knows
the way, he eh go let you lost –
both of you going the same way, don't it?

        Something
in these alley-shapes, the dark, the scratch
of foot-step pause a matchflare
catching the bass bearded voice within
the circle in the yard, within
the sweet smell of smoke saying:
peace and love, mi I-dren, peace and love

         Something of all this
stretches inside your sinews till they become guitar strings
trengling under the chop-and-slash
of fingers ratcheting at chords that cry, like
when love hurts you, like
when a lean, lost alley-cat, twisting in her heat
starts wailing:
      skeng-ek
      skeng-ek
      skenk-ek

ANTONETTE'S BOOGIE

i could do wid one o' dem boogie tonight
a deepdown spiritual chanting rising upfull-I
a Bunny Wailer flailing Apollyon with a single song
i could be in a mystic dance tonight
when every tramp I tramp I stamp de dragon head down into hell
and every high step lifting my leg one more rung upon de Jacob ladder
and dark as de place be, it have a light
it have a light, sweet Jah, more beautiful than fire!

i miss dat kinda boogie tonight
where your heartbeat is de bass-line
and everything so still within de centre of de music
although to an outsider it sound noisy
but doh mind, out dere is de wilderness
and here alone in dis place is de voice of prophecy
wailing in de reggae ridim for our time

telling us to flee, to forward, doh look back
and wo! right in de middle of de song
Bob singing stop – de rams' horns start to wail
and dis dance-hall is an ark
dis dance become a journey

One o' dem kinda dance i want
where flesh to flesh is serious business
where de rubber and de dubber making one
a dance where music is priest
and de deejay from de tribe of Levi
and all our voices from de valley of de dance floor
rise up in jubilation everywhere upspringing children of Jah
chanting psalm unto psalm unto psalm unto psalm
night into morning, praising and raising every heart higher
until de light
and den we sight Jah face

i miss dat kinda boogie tonight
where de dance-hall is a holy place.

"SO JAH SEY"

Dread song. "Not one of my seed" the words said
(and it hurt every time i heard Bob sing)
"shall sit on your sidewalk and beg your bread."
No, Pa, i'd think, never. My eyes would sting.
And yet it could have happened. Easily.
i burned to live a different kind of life,
more wild, more free – in fact, the kind that he
had lived, even with children and a wife.
My simmering rage would boil sometimes, would spurt
hot scalding words on him. i'd almost leave.
But i knew he'd turn beggar. And that hurt.
Why? Pride? The thought that when he died i'd grieve?
No. But somehow he had become my son,
my seed. And i, a tree now, couldn't run.

AUDREY INGRAM ROBERTS

POEM II
for Duckie Simpson of "Black Uhuru"

Well charged, halfway between generations
of impotent anger and languid nonchalance,
you smile at the irony that "I' n I are lazy"
for it took all your yesterdays of industry
to middle the passage between Rema and Jungle.

So long Rastafari call you, yet here you recline
with affected ease, locksed in the barrel of
Babylonian markets, captive to strategy.
So long you'd been away from home and the problems
of travel from Waterhouse to Constant Spring.
Now, bucking the pass, too grassed to fear the
youths of Englington spawned in violence,
or the duppy gunmen, uniformed for crime.

Well charged, you bus' it pon Red, free,
spaced out in raw control, Uhuru dread in
Babylon, Ja, Paris, London!
Sponged in reggae, seeped deep in pungent herbs
I glide above the undulating hills to see you
reach beyond with deft assurance and grasp a
life outside the violence that spawned you.

Well charged, I watch you grow, trusting that
you too, like Cliff, Marley, Toots, will show
another way to the coke ruptured youths obedient
to the orders of the remington.
Hard of hearing above the cacophony of nothing
to lose or gain, in the violence that spawned them.

BONGO JERRY

MABRAK

lightning
is the future brightening,
for last year man learn
how to use black eyes.
(wise!)

Mabrak:
          NEWSFLASH!
"Babylon plans crash"
Thunder interrupt their programme to
announce:
BLACK ELECTRIC STORM
                    IS HERE
How long you feel "fair to fine
(WHITE)" would last?

How long calm in darkness
          when out of BLACK
          came forth LIGHT?

How long dis slave caste
          when out of
          the BLACK FUTURE
comes
          I
          RIGHTS
          ?

Every knee
          must bow

Every tongue
        confess
Every language
        express
        W
        O
        R
        D
        W
        O
        R
        K
        S
YOU
        MUST
                COME
to RAS

MABRAK
Enlightening is BLACK
hands writing the words of
black message
for black hearts to feel.

Mabrak is righting the wrongs and brain-whitening – HOW?
Not just by washing out the straightening and wearing dashiki t'ing:

MOSTOFTHESTRAIGHTENINGISINTHETONGUE - so HOW?
Save the YOUNG
from the language that MEN teach,
the doctrine Pope preach
skin bleach.

HOW ELSE?. . . . . MAN must use MEN language
                to carry dis message:

SILENCE BABEL TONGUES; recall and
recollect BLACK SPEECH.

Cramp all double meaning
         an' all that hiding behind language bar,

for that crossword speaking
         when expressing feeling

is just English language contribution to increase confusion in
         Babel-land tower —

delusion, name changing, words rearranging
         ringing rings of roses, pocket full of poses:

"SAR" instead of "RAS"

left us in a situation
         where education
mek plenty African afraid, ashamed, unable to choose
         (and use)

BLACK POWA. (Strange Tongue)

NOT AGAIN!
Never be the same!
Never again shame!

Ever now communicate — for now I and I come to recreate:
sight sounds and meaning to measure the feeling
of BLACK HEARTS — alone —

MABRAK: frightening
MABRAK: black lightning

The coming of light to the black world: Come show I the way,
come make it plain as day — now — come once, and come for all
           and every one better come to RAS
for I come far, have far to go from here:

for the white world must come to blood bath
and blood bath is as far as the white world can reach; so when MABRAK
start skywriting,
LET BABYLON BURN
JEZEBEL MOURN
LET WEAK HEART CHURN
BLACK HOUSE STAND FIRM: for somewhere under ITYOPIA rainbow,
AFRICA WAITING FOR I.

LINTON KWESI JOHNSON

BASS CULTURE
(for Big Yout)

1
muzik of blood
black reared
pain rooted
heart geared

all tensed up
in di bubble an di bounce
an di leap an di weight-drop

it is di beat of di heart
this pulsing of blood
that is a bubblin bass
a bad bad beat
pushin gainst di wall
whey bar black blood

an is a whole heappa
passion a gather
like a frightful form
like a righteous harm
giving off wild like is madness

2
BAD OUT DEY

3
hotta dan di hites of fire
livin heat doun volcano core
is di cultural wave a dread people deal

spirits riled
an rise an rail thunda-wise
latent powa
in a form resemblin madness
like violence is di show
burstin outta slave shackle
look ya! boun fi harm di wicked

man feel
him hurt confirm
man site
destruction all aroun
man turn
love still confirm
him destiny a shine lite-wise
soh life tek the form whey shiff from calm
an hold di way of a deadly storm

5
culture pulsin
high temperature blood
swingin anger
shattering di tightened hold
the false hold
round flesh whey wail freedom
bitta cause a blues
cause a maggot suffering
cause a blood klaat pressure
yet still breedin love
far more mellow
than di soun of shapes
chanting loudly

6
SCATTA-MATTA-SHATTA-SHACK!
what a beat!

7
for di time is nigh
when passion gather high
when di beat jus lash
when di wall mus smash
an di beat will shiff
as di culture alltah
when oppression scatta

REGGAE SOUNDS

Shock-black bubble-doun-beat bouncing
rock-wise tumble-doun soun music
foot-drop find drum blood story
bass history is a moving
                is a hurting black story

Thunda from a bass drum sounding
lightning from a trumpet and a organ
bass and rhythm and trumpet double-up
team-up with drums for a deep doun searching

Rhythm of a tropical electrical storm
(cooled doun to the pace of the struggle)
flame-rhythm of historically yearning
flame-rhythm of the time of turning
measuring the time for bombs and for burning

Slow drop. make stop. move forward.
dig doun to the root of the pain
shape it into violence for the people
they will know what to do they will do it

Shock-black bubble-doun-beat bouncing
rock-wise tumble-doun soun music
foot-drop find drum blood story
bass history is a moving
                is a hurting black story

FIVE NIGHTS OF BLEEDING
(*for Leroy Harris*)

1
madness…madness…
madness tight on the heads of the rebels
the bitterness erupts like a hot-blast
                broke glass
rituals of blood on the burning
served by a cruel in-fighting
five nights of horror an of bleeding
                broke glass
cold blades as sharp as the eyes of hate
an the stabbings
it's war amongst the rebels
madness…madness…war.

2
night number one was in BRIXTON
SOPRANO B sound system
was a beating out a rhythm with a fire
coming doun his reggae-reggae wire
it was a soun shaking doun your spinal column
a bad music tearing up your flesh
an the rebels them start a fighting
the yout them jus turn wild
it's war amongst the rebels
madness…madness…war.

3
night number two doun at SHEPHERD'S
right up RAILTON ROAD
it was a night named Friday
when everyone was high on brew
or drew a pound or two worth a kally
soun coming doun NEVILLE KING'S music iron
the rhythm jus bubbling an back-firing
raging an rising, then suddenly the music cut
steel blade drinking blood in darkness
it's war amongst the rebels
madness…madness…war.

4
night number three
over the river
right outside the RAINBOW
inside JAMES BROWN was screaming soul
outside the rebels were freezing cold
babylonian tyrants descended
pounced on brothers who were bold
so with a flick
of the wrist
a jab an a stab
the song of blades was sounded
the bile of oppression was vomited
an two policemen wounded
righteous righteous war.

5
night number four at a blues dance
                    a blues dance
two rooms packed an the pressure pushing up
hot. hot heads. ritual of blood in a blues dance
                                    broke glass

splintering fire, axes, blades, brain — blast
rebellion rushing doun the wrong road
storm blowing doun the wrong tree
an LEROY bleeds near death on the fourth night
                                    in a blues dance
on a black rebellious night
it's war amongst the rebels
madness…madness…war.

6
night number five at the TELEGRAPH
vengeance walked through the doors
so slow
so smooth
so tight an ripe an smash!
                        broke glass
a bottle finds a head
an the shell of the fire-hurt cracks
the victim feels fear
                finds hands
                holds knife
                finds throat
o the stabbings an the bleeding an the blood
it's war amongst the rebels
madness…madness…war.

JANE KING

INTERCITY DUB
for Jean

Brixton groans —
From the horror of the hard weight
Of history
Where the whites flagellate
In their ancestry
And the blacks hold the stone
And they press it to their hearts
And London is a hell
In many many parts.
But your voice rings true
From the edge of hell
Cause the music is the love
And you sing it so well.

And I travel through the country
On the inter-city train
And the weather may be bad
But the sperm of the rain
Wriggles hope, scribbles hope
Cross the windows of the train
And the autumn countryside
Has a green life still
And the rain-sperm says
It will come again, it will
It will come again
New rich life from the bitter
And dark and driving rain —
And you run like water
Over Brixton soil
Writing hope on the windows

Bringing light through the walls
Like the water you connect
With the light above
Like the water writing making
The green life swell
Cause the music is the love
And you sing it so well.

Now I cannot give to you
What you gave to me
But one small part
Of your bravery
Makes me stand up to say
That I want to make them see
That you showed me the way
That the way is you
And the way is we.
And the love is in the water
In the wells pooled below
And the love is in the light
And the rain lances down
From the light to the well
And it points to heaven
And it points to hell
And the love is real
Make the music swell
Cause the music is the love
And you sing it so well.

There's a factory blowing smoke-rings
Cross the railway line
You know it took me time to learn
That this country wasn't mine
And I want to go back home
To swim in the sunset bay
Feel the water and the light

Soft-linking night and day
Like the music makes a bridge —
But there's joy here too
And I might not have seen it
If I hadn't heard you.
And I hope now I'll be writing
This poem all my life
For the black city world
Where the word is a knife
That cuts through the love
And divides up the life.
For you saved me from a trap
Just before I fell
Cause the music is the love
And you sing it so well.

The Brixton-battered sisters
Hissed their bitterness and hate
With their black man the oppressor
And death the white race fate
And they don't want to build
No bridge no gate —
And I nearly turned back
Till I heard your voice
Ringing clarion-clear
And you burst like a flower
From the sad sad soil
And you blew like a breeze
Round the shut-tight hall
And you danced like a leaf
And you sang like a bell —
You said Music reaches heaven
And music changes hell
Cause the music is the love
And you sing it so well.

DOROTHY WONG LOI SING

BAAP-NEMESTHE REGGAE SONG

Baap, nemesthe,
Maam, nemesthe,
Widya says when she is
coming home from school.
Bhai, kaha?
Aaaaaah, nana!
Oooh, accha!
That's fine ....

I saw and heard
such a crazy thing
coming home by bus,
Maam,
there was a young Black girl
with snakes in her hair
and a little Chinese drum:
Rom – tie tum!

She was drumming all the way
from home to school
– What a fool! –
Said she had a message
to all of us:
tom – ta tom
playing on her drum
She said
the Time had come
– bom-ba-bom –
to bring all the peoples to Unity
in the whole wide world.

Young and Old
so she told,

of all kinds of races,
of all kinds of tongues,
of all kinds of colours
ta-ta-tam-tam —

She cried out loud!
'Wooooey! Follow me please,
and sing, and shout,
and spread the News,
like Me!'

You know what's strange, Maam?
She could speak all tongues!
Hindi, Sarnami, Sranan,
Trurkish, Dutch, and a bit from Japan,
Russian, Bahasa Indonesia, Chinese, African
languages, even the secret religious ones!
She could sing in Spanish too
and in Antillean Papiamentu.

German, French, Swedish,
Moroccan tongues, more than I can
count or know about
(being only fifteen years old)
So little Widya told
her parents
She became a little insecure
and asked: 'Can it be true?
Maam? Baap?'

'Accha, larki,
that's real good news!
We're sure it's true!

It will be true!
It's good, it's good!
Accha!'

Y se quedaran los pajaros, cantando...
and birds were singing heavenly
to you and me
everywhere on this tiny planet Earth.

MALACHI

PSALM OF SILK

The Prophet stood
opened his heart
and chanted from the mountain top
of Jam Rock
songs of silk
sermons of redemption
to the dry bones
buried alive
in iniquity
he chanted

a man is just a man
a man is just a man

The prophet chanted
psalms of silk
look to the East
a black king cometh
Christ in his king character
one love it must be Jah Jah
who rules it for iver

a man is just a man

The prophet chanted to the morning
he chanted to the evening
to the rocks
songs of silk
like a quilt
cocooned the bones

warming their souls
filling them

They danced
they glowed
like poinsettias
down in Jamaica

a man is just a man
a man is just a man

Like Bob and Peter
Jacob Killah Miller
Don Drummond, Count Ossie
Joe Ruglass, Mikey Smith
Hugh Mundell
time alone will tell......

The prophet saw Zion in a vision
Mama Africa stretching out her hand
the dry bones could not understand
but like Elijah of old
Garnet Silk was raptured
out of Babylon.

AHDRI ZHINA MANDIELA

MIH FEEL IT
(Wailin fih Mikey)

Dih dred ded
an it dun suh?
No sah

di dred ded
an it dun suh?

    Ow can a man
    kill annadah one
    wid stone
    cold-
    bludded intenshan

    rockstone
    bludgeon im ead
    an
    im drop dung ded
    an nuh one
    nuh awsk
    why
    such a wikkid
    wikkid tawsk
    should
    anna-
    nyah-
    late
    dih dred

Di dred ded
an it dun suh?

no sah

di dred ded
an it dun suh?

Early early
inna dih day
Mikey ah trod
dung a illy way
isite up sum men
from a pawty fence
an hence-
forth
was stopped!
wid all dih
chattin whe gwaan
an questions ensued
Mikey painin run out
ah im mout
too soon!
an is den dih trouble
run out

for BAM!
four stone inna dem ans
an BAM!
dem lik Mikey dung
an
mih feel it
mih feel it
mih feel it

Dih dred ded an it dun suh?
no sah
dih dred ded
an it dun suh?

ones must know
dih reasons
for dis deadly
assault
committed
out of season
no reason
dred dred dred dred
season

'Riddemshan for every dred
mus come
riddemshan
mus cum'

is dih livity
not dih rigidity
for even doah seh
Mikey ded
cause dem mash up
im ead
even doah seh
Mikey gawn
im spirit trod awn
trod awn
tru: RIDDEMSHAN

'Riddemshan for every dred
mus cum
riddemshan
mus cum'
Dih dred ded
an it dun suh?'
NO SAH!

SPESHAL RIKWES

speshal rikwes
to dih ilan possie
for babbilan still ah try ole I
awndah slavery

ah membah wen
chain shackle I foot
now ah men-made leddah wintah boot
an in times before
men in a klan
cum wid dem plan
fih mash dung I state
as man an ooman
but I naw guh back
an dwell pan pass attacks
instead I ah mek a fahwud check
wid dis
speshal rikwes

speshal rikwes
from a yearnin ungah
burning burnin
burnin in dih mind of
of a city-bred yout
speshal rikwes fih dih trute

speshal rikwes
fih dih bones in dih sands
of dih Carrybeyan lands
fih wih urtin spirits debri
speshal rikwes fih you
an fih me

fih dih skills
of dih uprooted ones
widout birtlan
wukkin fih fahrin investment plans
inna Merrica, Sout Afrikka
Cannada an Inglan
inna dis yah babbilan

speshal rikwes fih I lan

fih dih blud ah dih eart
dih sawff red dirt
dat we fawt to preserve
fih wih own pots of clay
while dem watch evvy day
an say: MEK DEM PAY! MEK DEM PAY!
suh ow now I mus res
from makin dis
speshal rikwes?

wen dem ah try dem bes
fih keep I awndah stress
an covah dung I success
wid dem IQ tes
usin dem bans an bans
ah propaganda wagons
from dih still-bawn creashan
of dem feeble ans

but yuh know
sumting gawn wrong
wid dem plan
for look: I still ah stan strong
an I ah call to all ones
(fih elp clean up dih mess)

wid dis
speshal rikwes

speshal rikwes
espeshally
fih dih natives
sedated an apathy-stated
by apawtide: all roun dih worl

for apawt from I
dem hide/ dem hide
an seek fih mek I weak
but since JAH bless I
wid strent
fih strive an relent
I wih stan up an projek
forevah dis speshal rikwes

speshal rikwes fih dih ilan possie
speshal rikwes fih you an fih me

RACHEL MANLEY

BOB MARLEY'S DEAD
(For Drum)

The moon is full
heavy yellow
Marley's dead
and there is prophecy

Hallelujah
Jah is singing on the moon
and all our pain
is like the shadow of a branch
across its face;
it's not the King who lives
long live the King
it is the Kingdom lives

My island is a mother
burying wombs
I rise, at my beginning
the squalor
the flower

The moon is dread
she bleeds
Marley's dead
and there is prophecy

The Kingdom lives
a heart of drums
a small town throbs,
we have begun
the phoenix

from a mulch of bones
I rise beyond
a fantasy
I wake
I break faith
with the white dream

The moon is black
my mother sings with me
Oh Marley's dead
and there is prophecy.

MARC MATTHEWS

BY A WAYS

By a ways through mento prayers,

midnight   bluebeat   riddum
an' reggae,
Jimmy Cliff
"Sitting here in limbo
faith
leading me on
leading me on"

Sea of history
breaking
on the windows
of the 176 bus,
Caribbean to
Greater Brixton
1989.

Is just so
time stan'
not no ticking of tock
but loud falling sun
blinding through shadowed
Auld Lang Syne
to remind:
eighteen hundred
an twenty.

Can hear firm last stanza
echo   calm
of dignity

inscribe tomb
on burdened unblessed stone
beaching waves of feet

From always where rasping ocean
files volcanic stone
foaming endlessly
sermons of sand
recycled into concrete floors
supporting a bottom shelf
– literature of cardboard
homes between bookends –
of County and Festival Halls.

Sea of history
breaking
on the windows
of 176 Liverpool Street
to Greater Brixton
1989.

Hear William Davidson's
righteous scorn upon
this cemetery of horse power
and history's foul dung-tipped scales
of justice, favouring
vulture-taloned commerce.

A way,
once opon a penalty framed
Newgate appears where
Old Bailey stands
beside congealed blood, saturated
concrete, shadowed city artery
paved with the forgotten sounds
of bound soles' scuffling side
walk, by a ways.

Is just so
time stan'
not so ticking of tock
but loud falling sun
blinding through 169 shadowed
years to Auld Lang Syne

Sea of history
breaking
on the windows
of the 176 bus
Greater Brixton to
Clapham Junction
1989.

LANGUAGE

Dis is one recitation
one declaration
dat ketch it riddum
from man empty belly drum
'oman dry up bubbie.
Sufferation na come
in couplets
metaphor nor allegory
it lan' by community
by family.

When me pickney
ketch feva
dem belly swell
dem mout boast
white carna
me woman, me mudda

cyan stan' up fuh
pressure.
Me still a watch
fuh structcha?

If ah shop pon corna
na gie awee trus',
wha mex say
dem a go tek
iambic pentameter
an doh awee is
born a same country,
some awee neva understan'
mattie.
Yuh deh ah talk poetry
me stan heh an talk
plain, plain poverty.

MBALA

A NEW DUB

ah tink it's time:
fi
tear it dung
tek it to pieces
an put it back togedda diffrantly

time fi tek dis smood
seamless ting
an mek supp'm
wid di joints showing
elbows knees
angles glinting di lite from yu eyes
into a million diffrant directions

supp'm dat wont
slipslide outa yu han
an bounce (harmlessly) pan di floor

hard
but not supp'm mek outa metal

time:
fi supp'm yu can put togedda
inna yu backyard
widout flanger or sequencer or phillips
head screwdriva
widout factry
wid essence of dent an
mash finga
an dirt
an a piece a yu soul

THE HISTORY OF DUB POETRY

di sun si it all aready
from flappin dadaist
to dub poet
amusin bemusin
confusin di centre
from griot to
rockin minstrel rollin into court
an village
wile wid laaf an colour
dancehallin towards yu conscience
an yu hardly
feel di barb
as di bard
slip it to yu
thru di space dem
between yu laafta
as slow an invisible
ova centries
di rapso man
calypso man
sad yu
laaf yu
to tears dat melt weh yu walls
an di sun si it all
again
burnin thru
slang and syntax
thru di dub of
tabla an cello an talkin drum
as di bline chanta
in di artic ice
bogle wid a piece a
holy blubba
and

plug een
electric
to supp'm wid
whole heap a name an no name
an di snow sun
di desert sun
di sun si it all again
flappin dadaist
dub poet
amusin
bemusin
confusin
dancehallin
towards yu soul

ANTHONY MCNEILL

SAINT RAS

Every stance seemed crooked. He had
not learned to fall in with the straight
queued, capitalistic, for work.
He was uneasy in traffic.

One step from that intersection
could, maybe, start peace. But he dread-
fully missed, could never proceed
with the rest when the white signal

flashed safe journey. Bruised, elbowed-in
his spirit stopped at each crossing,
seeking the lights for the one sign
indicated to take him across

to the true island of Ras.
But outside his city of dreams
was no right-of-passage, it seemed.
Still-anchored by faith, he idled

inside his hurt harbour and even
his innocent queen posed red
before his poised, inchoate bed.
Now exiled more, or less,

he retracts his turgid divinity,
returns to harsh temporal streets
whose uncertain crossings reflect
his true country. Both doubt and light.

ODE TO BROTHER JOE

Nothing can soak
Brother Joe's tough sermon,
his head swollen
with certainties.

When he lights up a s'liff
you can't stop him,
and the door to God, usually shut,
gives in a rainbow gust.

Then it's time for the pipe,
which is filled with its water base
and handed to him for his blessing.
He bends over the stem,
goes into the long grace,
and the drums start

the drums start
Hail Selassie I
Jah Rastafari,
and the room fills with the power
and beauty of blackness,
a furnace of optimism.

But the law thinks different.
This evening the Babylon catch
Brother Joe in his act of praise
and carry him off to the workhouse.

Who'll save Brother Joe? Hail
Selassie is far away
and couldn't care less,
and the promised ship

is a million light years
from Freeport.

But the drums in the tenement house
are sadder than usual tonight

and the brothers suck hard
at their s'liffs and pipes:
Before the night's over
Brother Joe has become a martyr;

But still in jail;
And only his woman
who appreciates his humanness more
will deny herself of the weed tonight
to hire a lawyer
and put up a true fight.

Meantime, in the musty cell,
Joe invokes, almost from habit,
the magic words:
Hail Selassie I
Jah Rastafari,
But the door is real and remains shut.

FOR THE D
"To John Coltrane, the heaviest spirit"
– Inscription, *Black Music*, Leroi Jones/Imamu Baraka

DON

may I learn the shape of that hurt
which captured you nightly into
dread city, discovering through
streets steep with the sufferer's beat;

Teach me to walk through jukeboxes
& shadow that broken music
whose irradiant stop is light;
guide through those mournfullest journeys

I back into harbour Spirit
in heavens remember me now
& show we a way in to praise I,
all seekers to-gather, one-heart:

and let we lock conscious when wrong
& Babylon rock back again:
in the evil season sustain
o heaviest spirit of sound.

BOB MARLEY NEW KING OF THE MUSIC

bob marley new king of the music
behind him don d

lovely an aching
chilling the bone

the moon-flower
is down

_____

i tell you all words are lovely
mostly

clichés

_____

it is light and air
that weaves music

watch it
you might go up

in smoke
prophet

going up
in the swing

you come down

————————————

a great poet black
don't spoil the party

make me spill mi dink
a great poet black

think of the force
in that name

where the worlds meet

————————————

if you love language
leave it alone

it's perfectly capable of giving you all
i thought everyone died for the project

like me
if so

they are not leaving
the line to turn

————————————

BRIAN MEEKS

THE TWIN BARREL BUCKY: A KINGSTON 12 DUB

is a
spring
loaded
sperm   out a
spewing   dialect-   through
high tension   ic line   the
wire   pours   undergrowth
on i   down a   of i
titerope   gunmetal   mind
of time/   riddim   the e-
watching   knows   masculated
the gas   no reso-   bull
leak out   lution   feudal-
the lifeline   the shot: izes
the yet   with lead   yesterday's
unborn   is said   sunset
the yet   you're as   the nite
unborn   good as   knew no
the father   dead   end an
figure   with a   the people
shines his   bucky   hid in
lovelite   in you   smoky
out on i   head   places
the trigger: if you   daily
blu steel   aint red   for
heals no   red red   it was
wounds   redder dan   tole
       hisses   red   they say
sweats   (mus dread)   a beast
                   the barrel: was at
                   waiting   loose
                   creeping   an known
                                     to be
                                     jumpy sometimes

IS CULCHA WEAPON?

can jamrock
rock out
        buckshot
shootin
jukebox souns
an beggin
for a
        ten cent
dread
for one
more stick
a lil?

will
        jamrock rock
walk naked
on fridays
    sundays
too   never
sleep   hunt
out the beast
haunt
its thoughts
nightly
fuck his
wife on
orange st shake
out his
lion dread
faint biznessmen
outside sheraton
fart freely?

can
        jamrock rock
crash down
a bev
        hill
                side
retainin wall

smash plate
                        glass
                torture
                                concrete
heated headlights
crack the esso
sign   bend
the stoplite
signal red is
go   piss
upon the
green baize desk?

does
        jamrock rock
know you
            will
it shoot too
if you dont
see through
this number?
weepin an a wailin
picks you up
an spins you
roun   doesnt
want to see
you dance
jus bus
dis shot
an pick
de lock   swing de
small axe   never
sleep awhile
on sundays
while   waitin   timely
once again
we smile

MARCH 9 1976

in a pack
dance hall
when de jump
is on
an' de muted
dub want to
eat itself
an de wood root
mix wid de
sweet scent a
ili
an de bass note
stop de idrens from
flyin'
not a man tek
notice a de
yellow cortina
an de five wrench
faces inside...

circlin' 'roun'
a Burnin' Spear
number, machine gun
mentalities
centered on tripes,
everyone check
when de clappers
firs' start
dat Burnin' Spear
riddim gon
wil'...

when de fire
stop bu'n
an who nuh reach
groun' scale de

wall an de gully
outside, five
wrenches remain'
an' one lead
spattered martyr
awaitin' his medal
behin'.

down Duke st.'s
closed bound-
aries crew cut
accountant
ticks off a
number/ closes
the doors
on a stars and
stripes file.

could the golf
caddy know
who fired his life
inspired this crime
'gainst the youth
of the town?

cryin' i sight
brown grass
of a city
trying to out
dry flames
with i tears.

300 miles
away
Uncle Sam
smiles.

PAM MORDECAI

JESUS IS CONDEMNED TO DEATH
from De Man

NAOMI:
Oonu see mi dyin trial!
Dem people yah nuh easy.
A kill dem a go kill de man.
How yuh mean "Which man?"
Nuh de man Jesus. Yuh know –
de one dat preach? And
Tell story? Yuh never hear
Him yet? Bwoy, me nuh
Understand oonu young
People. If oonu did stay at
Oonu yard, me would seh
Come. But oonu walk street
And ignorant same way.
Me studying dis man from
Him come down a Jordan side
And mek de Baptist dip him.
Is dat baptism yuh must
Hear about! Dat's how
Me know is not a ting but
Politricks – dat and red eye.
All dem old hypocrite –
Seh dem is priest and nuh
Have time fi people.
A good ting rain nuh fall
Fi joke round dese parts else
Dem would a sure fi drown.
So dem ugly, a so de man
Good-looking. Dem have big
Word fi t'row but him

Could talk. De truth is not
A one o' dem could draw
A crowd like him. And when
Him ready him just tek
Time and do a likl healing:
Who lame cyan walk. Who dumb
Cyan talk... Dem seh him all
Raise dead! Beelzebub
Or no Beelzebub –
De man have power yuh hear.
Dem old and ugly, full
Up of dem self; have nuff book
Learning and cyaan talk three
Word straight. And if dem life
Did turn pon it dem wouldn't
Have de power fi mek
A dead fish twitch.
Dat is de whole ting –
Cash bill and receipt.
So dem send some old
Criminal fi drape him up
And drag him here. Real
Ragamuffin – if yuh
Ever see dem... Beg yuh just
Pass mi head-wrap – do. Time
Going. Me betta go dere quick.
God know which dutty business
Dem a knock dem wicked head
Togadda fi perpetrate...

Is must be why my mistress send
Me to report on what dem
Doing to him. Me sure she not
Going stand fi it. Me hear
Her tell de Pilate one
"You let him die and you

Will have no peace." She seh
She dream some awful tings
And yuh know dat is one
Could dream...
                    Still
Pray Jah dat my future
Never rest with that frog-
Face for him have neither
Character nor courage
Nor de commonsense
Fi do what him wife seh.

MERVYN MORRIS

VALLEY PRINCE
(for Don D.)

Me one, way out in the crowd,
I blow the sounds, the pain,
but not a soul
would come inside my world
or tell me how it true.
I love a melancholy baby,
sweet, with fire in her belly;
and like a spite
the woman turn a whore.
Cool and smooth around the beat
she wake the note inside me
and I blow me mind.

Inside here, me one
in the crowd again,
and plenty people
want me to blow it straight.
But straight is not the way; my world
don' go so; that is lie.
Oonu gimme back me trombone, man:
is time to blow me mind.

RASTA REGGAE
(for The Mystics)

out of that pain
that bondage
heavy heavy sounds

our brothers' weary march
our shackled trip

a joyful horn takes off
to freedom time
remembered and foretold

Release I brother let me go
let my people go
home to Ethiopia
in the mind

FOR CONSCIOUSNESS

Ol' plantation wither,
factory close down,
brothers of de country
raisin' Cain in town.

An' now dem in de city
sweatin' blood dem fin'
is jus' like de same system
dem mean to lef' behin':

but agents of de owners dem
is harder now to sight –
plenty busha doan ride horse
an' some doan t'ink dem white.

In de new plantation story
firs' t'ing dat have to know
is who an' who to tackle
when de call to battle blow.

GRACE NICHOLS

BEVERLEY'S SAGA
(For Beverley and Jamaican dub-poet, Jean Binta Breeze)

Me good friend Beverley
Come to England. She was three.
She born in Jamaica, but seh,
Dis ya she country.
She ancestor blood help fe build it,
Dat is history.
Dih black presence go back
Two, three century.

She seh she fadder
Was minding he own business
Back in Jam-country,
Wid he lickle piece-o-land
An he lickle donkey
When dey sen he fe enlist
In de British Army.
Yes, he hads was to fight
Fe dis ya country.
Dey even give he medal fe bravery.

So policeman na come
Wid no brutality.
Mister Repatriation, yuh know,
You will haffi kill she
Cause she na go no whey
Dis ya she country.
Summer is hearts
An she dread de wintry
But she have she lickle flat
An she have she lickle key.
She seh she like it fine
She a pop wid style
You can never put she back inna no woodpile
Or she bun it to de ground.

She seh she went to Uncle Sam
For a six week vacation,
But after three week
She homesick fe England.
When de plane mek a touch-down
She feel so happy,
She feel she a come home,
Dis ya she country.
If dey think about repatriation
Dem will haffi kill she.

De odder day
Wan ole English lady stop she,
Seh, 'Miss are you on holiday?'
Bev seh, 'Me not on holiday,
Me a live right hey.
Me na plan fe go no whey.'

De ole lady open she eye, suprisedly,
Bev seh, 'Is Black British dey call we.'
She seh, 'I don't mean to be unkind
But leh me tell you lickle history –
You see all dis big fat architectry?
In it is de blood of my ancestry.
Dih black presence go back
Two, three century.
Don't look at me so bemusedly.'

Bev seh, 'In any case, you been my country first,
So we come back inna kinda reverse.
Isn't life funny? Dis ya. Dis ya history.
O mek we tek a lickle walk,
It so nice an sunny.
Summer is hearts,
An a dread de wintry.
But a have me lickle flat
An a have me lickle key.
You want to come in
For a lickle cup-o-tea?'

OPAL PALMER ADISA

ETHIOPIA UNDA A JAMAICAN MANGO TREE

Jah Brown si-down
unda a mango tree
him anger
jus swell.

Babylon refuse
him wuk
cause him dreadlocks.

Him pull pon de weed
iflect Babylon gwine
meet fire I an I
son of Jah
I an I a guh
plough I land
I an I a guh eat fresh
vegetable no deadas. I an I
a guh mek dis mango tree
I temple. I an I a guh hook
till Jah come fi I.

But Jah Brown
nah frown,
cut no strut
weed cool him down.
Him eyes lost in smoke.

Ethiopia! Ethiopia! Ethiopia!
Ring in him ears
Jah Brown arrives at
Haile Sellasie's palace

Is given red cloak,
fresh fruits,
marries a queen.
Him spirit
soar.

Jah Brown wipe spittle
from him chin.
Raised arms held to
de sky,
"I an I is son of Jah
I an I is Jah
I an I is Prince among Princes
I an I is."

Jah Brown nah
cut no strut
him just si-down
unda Jah mango tree.

COUNT OSSIE

I saw you perform
your pearly smile
danced at me.
Mother Africa does well by her men
who keep close to her bosom

Now we speak of honour
we sing
but only you know de rhythm

Play Count Ossie
play de drums...

the telephone of Africa
play
while you journey home

De drums bawl out sufferation
dem rejoice, dem bawl
dem sound for you Count Ossie
Play de drums.

NO, WOMEN DON'T CRY

In Africa, the saying is:
"A man is nothing without a woman
he cannot be a chief and when his breath
leaves him, his name
will be knocked into the earth
forgotten as his flesh."

So we women don't cry
we carry pain
in our bosom,
our stomachs bulge
pregnated by sorrow
we guard our tears
like a dam
for if we were to shed one drop
we couldn't stop
and we wouldn't have been able
to fight the Portuguese in the Congo,
the English in the Portland hills of Jamaica or
prisoners and derelicts of Europe in the Americas

If just one salt
had run down our cheeks

the pyramids would not be built
and the 60 million Africans
who drowned, starved and were killed
in the usurption of the continent – the middle passage
would not even be a memory

So women don't cry
we don't cry
mothers don't cry
when their husbands creep through the back door
while they remain with a stone stare
to sing freedom in the enemy's face,
sisters don't cry
when they see their brothers
strung up mutilated,
daughters don't cry
when a moment's rape
alters their future
no, women don't cry
we just hold it in
the crevices of our teeth,
in our wombs,
under our arm pits
in the loops of our ears
we women don't cry
we only weep and wail
in our rocking
that's why we talk to ourselves
and build more lives.

GEOFFREY PHILP

HEIRLOOMS

Through the garbled signals
of a transistor radio
my mother kept for hurricanes like this,
but never like this,
we scan for the next location
of ice, water, food, and catch
the edge of a Caribbean tinged
station, fragments of a Marley tune,
"No woman, nuh cry, everything's
gonna be all right," and my son,
barely nine months, who cut a tooth
while Andrew gnawed through the Grove,
dances with his mother
by the glow of a kerosene lamp which,
preserved through airport terminals,
and garage sales, as the window
splintered and the house glittered
for a moment before the walls
fell flat, stood on the mantle
of the fireplace we never used.
In the midst of the rubble
these, our only heirlooms, bind us
against the darkness outside:
all that she could ever give,
all that we could ever pass on
or possess: this light, this music.

DANCE HALL

Man, mek me tell yu, dat was a fete.
Riddim was wile, an de dawta dem a grine,
De idren dem a smoke de sweetes lamb's bret
Straight from St. Ann's, de bes colly we cud fine.
Security did tight, yu cudn even see a rachet,
Fa de local top-ranking stan up broad by de gate
Till one fool-fool rumhead decide fe chuck a yute.
Buway, me neva see one man eat so much bullet.
We kotch de buway pon a speaka, an call him girl fren;
She search him till she fine de gole ring inna him ves,
An shub him dung a dutty, figet him like de res.
Now das when de dance like like it was guwane en,
Den we put on sum oldies, an leggo de bass,
Fa yu cyan cum a dance widdout a gun inna yu wais.

II

Dread beat reverb thru de centre;
Ityopian queens movin to a conscious beat:
A soun fe mash dung Babylon, bus de Pope heart,
A soun fe crush de plan of all backbiter
Who doan tink it too tough fe sell my skin,
Condemn me to dungle fe live inna mud;
Fill me wid disease and sell me blood
At a profit while dem save dem own.
But yout want a new soun, fas like hip-hop:
Speaker mus stammer like a M16 bark
An we ride synthesiza riddim till we drop.
De woman by yu side mus tear off her bra strap,
An wave her baggy in de air to all de slackness talk.
But yu tink she will be yu queen when de music stop?

DANCE HALL: VERSION

you see me dying trial, gun inna the dance:
after me wake up with crosses, gingy fly
round my head, like i was deaf, crosses inna me

bed like ants crawling over me chest, inna the yard
rubbing themself gainst the tamarind make me want
to fling this bag of bone like it worth a raas?

after light man lock off the fridge, spoil me food,
water man cut off the pipe, boss man meet me with soap
in me beard, evening find me clothes in a pothole

of mosquito, landlord padlock the door, change
the key, and all me come the dance is to sip some man-
ish water, rent-a-tile, clean the cobweb from the corner

of me brain while i hole a dawta, and slip
me hand over her warm breast with the sweet
smell of herb climbing up her skirt, and the one

thing on me mind is that the boots don't burst,
and sing in time with gregory isaacs, the cool
ruler on the turntable, yes, yes, yes.

ONE SONG

when dis ya bass-line drop
is like *rebel music* bus inna mi brain:

dew fall, leaf curl, riddim dat will neva stop;
when dis ya bass-line drop,

brother bob wails, *hey, mr. cop*:
shistem buckle when the word-sound reign;

when dis ya bass-line drop,
is like *rebel music* bus inna mi brain.

VELMA POLLARD

HEAVENS CHERUBIM HIGH HORSED
OR THE MEETING OF THE TWO SEVENS (MAY 1977)

Poised smiling on your charger
high striding on your stilts
my mokojumbie
god among gods
made flesh and carpenter
teacher and gardener
words man
sounds man
life man

I might have missed you
Mannnn
I might have missed
your vacant mystery look
collecting images
vibrations
I might have missed you
god!

You found me out
measured my acres
chose a site and
bam! implosed upon me
many mouthed concerns
onions azaleas
cows and compost heaps

I find my spirit dancing in my head
I find me whirling to your many strings
and do I see you spinning on your stilts

burning the pure glint of your steady eye
deepening the hollow angel fingers
pressed into your cheeks?

You feel I know
but something surely
smaller than my awe
you had no search
how then could you have found?

I sought a man
a black man with his head
still firmly stitched into his black resolve
no jiving teeny bopper
overgrown with time

I found you mokojumbie.
frightened... with faith I touch your rib
and spin again to scream
"It's real!"

ROHAN PRESTON

MUSIC

Burning Spear wails with a hole, a hollow, in his voice
a strained strain, taut from squeezing out the sound, de sound
de soun: *Marcus Garvey words come to pass.*
Tired of the echoes, Mau-Mau bawling from Mount Kenya,
tired of the waiting and politicians, shegries and lies:
See the hypocrites them a galong deh.

But a no so i fi go.

Burning Spear has a chasm in his voice –
not an abyss, mind you – but a big gap nonetheless
through which Nanny and Sam Sharpe, Harriet, Frederick
Toussaint and Eric Williams – the long train of Maroons
stream up; where Paul Bogle tells the colonial tribunal
(for him never did have any sort of fair hearing, you know)
tell today's jury, how them hang him for asking:
Am I not... But him couldn't go no further
"Black" and "Man" no fit too well in the same sentence
(*You favour flying patoo, you favour...*)
for that was the sentence, the missionary terms
for a Cain, canine.

Sister Nanny up there in Cockpit Country inventing guerrilla war-
fare and bleeding herself free of the plantation.
Them say she work obeah, pocomania and vodoun
them say a black magic, heathen whispers make her strong
make her catch bullets with her behind and fart them out.
But it beat back the British, no? If a poco make her 'trong
come work 'pon me, High Priestess, come sing
make the woofers loosen the knots/gnats/knots in my stomach
warm the showers every time Babylon glowers at me.

You see these little Caribbean islands sailing away,
sculpted like beautiful tourist postcards,
these little irregular punctuations in the sea
connected by vast amounts of salt and water
nutritious from the bones of the Middle Passage.

Do you remember the days of slavery?

These little lands created by blowing bubbles
no make them fool you – them too small
to contain the voices, too small to hold the history
think of the water instead.

Burning Spear has a hollow in his voice
the spirits too big for the media, cracking
spilling ancestors onto digital
harvest moon and jukwunu
exploding guts, tar, feather, cat-o-nine tails

But a no so i' fi go

When the rain stops falling down
And they ain't go no water
They're gonna bow down to the ground
Wishing that they were under

When the stars start falling off
And the fire is burning (red hot)
There will be a weeping and gnashing of teeth
At four in the morning

Hear the names of the dancehall dee-jays
Colonel Mite and Lieutenant Stitchie sewing up the wounds
Ninja Man and Daddy Lizard at Cross Roads
Shelley Thunder with the (small) double ax of Shango.

See the South African school children
girls in blue dresses, boys in khaki uniforms
dancing the toyi-toyi in the streets of Soweto
their feet trodding for grapes and vineyards
plotting a bitter wine.

Nelson free, Nelson free, we feel irie
Them free Mandela out a penitentiary

Deep, deep down in the diamond dunes
drilling, digging and drowning in dust
close to the stimela fields and all across
the hinterland, plowing the crenelated veldt
and feeling the master's sjambok wipe across
back and belly, back!back!back!
welting, wailing, draping them up
John Crow and rolling calf duppy
blap!blap!blap!

But a no so i' fi go

P.E. penultimate — all the voices coming out
squirming like worms, squeezed through telephone
and PA system: *Public Enemy Number One*
through the steel pipes of Rikers and Compton,
Spofford and Alcatraz — bloody ass, Babylon
the pimp, the warden smiles widely
there's weed growing among his teeth
may look like it, but the ancestor has not returned.

ITALIST CHANT

I can see buckra a come
Lock-step to start a fray
Coming with them chains and munitions
But I don't feel no way

Nesta Marley, Mosiah Garvey
A flow inna me vein
Malcolm X-mas, Luther Kingdom
Mash them down again

I can hear the missiles a hum
But Jah Jah a the conqueror
At Palmares, Addis Ababa
Duppyman conqueror

Harriet Tubman, King Shaka
Show Jah love for true
Sister Nanny, and Kenyatta
Pass their grace on to you

The one Hannibal, Nefertiti
All a them refuse to fall
Queen Mother and Mandibi
All of them are part a me

I can see the armies rolling
But Natty a the conqueror
For our fathers, foremothers
None of them a bangarang

I can hear the mountains calling
Jah Lion a the conqueror
Love you, Papa, love you, Mama
O, Zion a the conqueror

Final conka-conka-kang
Conka-conka-kang
Conka-conka-kang
Conka-conka-kang
Conqueror

DEEP-SEA BATHING
(Inna Reggae Dancehall)

Deep-sea bathing (inna reggae dancehall),
mish-mash, swoosh-splash, filling up
not only in a dead fish fashion.

Between each bass-blast
the woofers inhale like cartoon gods
ready to deliver one more blow.

The boomers gasp and pant with the plop
of a bobbing person every time
she pushes up, up, up above the waves,

so the bass dubs and dubs, body-batting
as if the wind were filling out hung clothes.
Deep-sea bathing, my round, settling

stomach makes hollows as if sweat
were peeling off of lovers' bellies,
my concentric rings fold over each other

like dewlap; and I begin to shake
them out, one by one, the way Mum taught
me when she ironed clothes.

CHAMPION CHANT

Yes, me bredren
O, me sistren –
Bread, Sis? Crisis – no cry, Sis

Yes, me bredren
And, me sistren (Sis)
Me bredren and me sistren not this shi-stem

Not these stealers
Crab-clawed dealers (ah-uh)
Putting on the hands of healers

But we know them
Godless children (true-true)
Want to open us up in post-mortem

Find what carried us
When they harried us (John Crow)
And rolled down the rocks to bury us

Called us ruffians
And hooligans (no, true)
And every blasted name in creation

True we a lions
'Trong-blood Africans (tell them)
All African lions are champions

Champion strivers
Campaign survivors (everytime)
Survive and thrive through their terrors

Through the laser guns
Bacterium (O, gosh)
And septic slosh sanitarium

So, come again now
For we nah bow (come no)
If you want fe buck, we show you how

Come all sistren
Come, all brethren
Every degge one of you a Jah-Jah children

Children of Zion
Teg-a-reg African
Every truthful fire is a champion.

TEN SECONDS

You have ten seconds
to pray, one to die,
to tear the wretchedness
out of your eyes –
just ten seconds, but
you need ten years
to strain some truth
from your reptile tears.

You beg, 'Dear, Father,
forgive me now
for raking them so
like dirt under plow,
I beg you, Father,
to anoint my cup' –
pram-pram, Babylon,
your prayer is up!

LLOYD RICHARDSON

THE POET SINGS HIS PAINTING

Neil Diamond
is
a pretty white boy —
as classically revolutionary as
America can get.

Marley
is
a dread
locks
that padlocks
and grips
the mind
in the forefront of
the struggle.

Diamond
has a rough
edge, tough
but rich,
which
speaks,
when smooth
of pigeons and seagulls, aaah,
in loving, poetic terms.

Limestone and Marl
ey is just as tough
as the earth:
hot,
so hot and so

                                        hungry
                                        that pigeons and seagulls
                                        do well to escape
                                        slingshots and stones
                                        before becoming bones
                                        squandered in gravy.

But the poet sings his song
and the people dance along
The Carpenters
have never built
a bench,
have never smelt
the stench of Trench
Town,
but sing in
glorious memory
of
"only yesterday".

                                        The Spear kills
                                        and burns
                                        and thrills,
                                        and the man in the hills
                                        oversees the land,
                                        from not too high up,
                                        sufficient to get
                                        the right perspective
                                        of the flight, prospective,
                                        only tomorrow.

When you listen
to Don
you know you're on
to the topping
of the U.S.A.
deejay.

"doo-dah
doo-dah"
is an American rhythm.

                            E.T.'s on the air
                            but down to earth
                            taking the people
                            to the land of their birth.
                            A little bit o' song
                            helps the people
                            to move along.
                            "bif, baf
                            bup, bip!!"
                            is a Jamdown
                            riddim.

And the poet sings his song
and the people dance along

Elton John
wears big glasses
and tight pants.

                            Judy Mowatt's eyes
                            wide open
                            and the biggest thing
                            the tightest thing
                            she got
                            breeds tomorrow's
                            struggler.

Erica Jong writes,
and the people are buying,
of the 'zipless fuck'
and the 'fear of flying'.

Check Miss Lou: and
the people are crying
for a need of food
and a fear of dying.

Shak
es
pe
a
re
(is that how you say it?)
wrote as you like it.
You didn't like it
but had to read,
study,
digest, congest,
fini
sh it,
before you could wear
the mark of the beast
upon your G.C.E.
cer
ti
fi
kit
(is that how you say it?)

Parboosingh paints
how
he like it.
You like it too.
But the little white tag
that's stuck on the painting
says the price is too high
and the wifey is waiting
to collect what is due,
so she,

nor you,
cannot understand
what the Parboosingh man
is saying.
And the writing's on the painting

And the poet sings his song
and the people dance along.

And even at home
the pot's not as black
as it's supposed to be;
or even like
the one
that made tea
in Britain.

At Creative Arts:
"You know I can't hear you when the water is running".

At the Barn:
"Skeleton's" fires rage and
the brothers are gunning.

At the Pegasus:
"If all that glitters"... aah, if only if...

While Nettleford's dancing
to the wailing of Cliff.

In schools:
"the benefits of speaking English speech".

While in "Smile Orange"
a brother licks out on de beach

At "Turntables":
the girlies gyrate to the Fatback Band

> In a little house in Rema:
> cho – Channel One.

And the poet sings his song
the singer writes his painting
the painter sings his poem
the poet sings his painting
the singer draws his poem

and whatever fuck
de whole a dem
dish out,
we
all
still
dance along

DENNIS SCOTT

APOCALYPSE DUB

At first, there's a thin, bright Rider —
he doesn't stop at the supermarket, the cool
red meats are not to his taste.
He steals from the tin on the tenement table,
he munches seed from the land
where no rain has fallen, he feeds
in the gutter behind my house.
The bread is covered with sores
when he eats it; the children
have painted his face on their bellies

The second rides slowly, is visiting, watch him, he smiles
through the holes in the roof
of the cardboard houses.
His exhaust sprays pus on the sheets,
he touches the women and teaches them
fever, he puts eggs under the skin —
in the hot days insects will hatch and hide
in the old men's mouths,
in the bones of the children

And always, behind them, the iceman, quick,
with his shades, the calm oil of his eyes —
when he throttles, the engine
grunts like a killer. I'm afraid,
you said. Then you closed the window
and turned up the radio, the DJ said greetings
to all you lovely people.
But in the street the children coughed like guns.

In the blueblack evenings
they cruise in the corner
giggling. Skenneng! Skenneng!

DREADWALK
for the Children

blackman came walking I
heard him sing his
voice was like sand
when the wind dries it

said sing for me dreamer
said blackman I cannot
the children are gone
like sand from the quarry

said are you afraid I
come closer said blackman
his teeth were like stone
where the pick cuts it

said do you remember
my mouth full of stones he said
give I the children
would not step aside

but you holding it wrong I
said love the fist opened
the knife fell away from
the raw hand middle

his voice was like wind
when the sea makes it salt
the sun turned a little
the shadows rolled flat
blowing closer afraid I
would not step aside

then he held me into
his patience   locked

one

now I sing for the children
like wind in the quarry
hear me now
by the wide torn places

I am walking.

MORE POEM

'No more poem!' he raged, eye red;
'A solitary voice is wrong,
Jericho shall fall, shall fall
at the People's song!'

So. Only I-tongue have the right
to reason, to that sense of dread.
Man must keep silence now, except
man without bread.

No. See the flesh? It is cave, it is
stone. Seals every I away from light.
Alone. Man must chant as Man can
gainst night.

OLIVE SENIOR

MEDITATION ON YELLOW

"The Yellow of the Caribbean seen from Jamaica
at three in the afternoon."
                    – Gabriel García Márquez

1

At three in the afternoon
you landed here at El Dorado
(for heat engenders gold and
fires the brain)
Had I known I would have
brewed you up some yellow fever-grass
and arsenic

but we were peaceful then
child-like in the yellow dawn of our innocence

so in exchange for a string of islands
and two continents

you gave us a string of beads
and some hawk's bells

which was fine by me personally
for I have never wanted to possess things
I prefer copper anyway
the smell pleases our lord Yucahuna
our mother Attabeira
It's just that copper and gold hammered into guanin
worn in the solar pendants favoured by our holy men
fooled you into thinking we possessed the real thing
(you were not the last to be fooled by our
patina)

As for the silver
I find that metal a bit cold
The contents of our mines
I would have let you take for one small mirror
to catch and hold the sun

I like to feel alive
to the possibilities
of yellow

lightning striking

perhaps as you sip tea
at three in the afternoon
a bit incontinent
despite your vast holdings
(though I was gratified to note
that despite the difference in our skins
our piss was exactly the same shade of yellow)

I wished for you
a sudden enlightenment that
we were not the Indies
nor Cathay
No Yellow Peril here
though after you came
plenty of bananas
oranges
sugar cane
You gave us these for our
maize
pineapples
guavas
– in that respect
there was fair exchange

But it was gold
on your mind
gold the light
in your eyes
gold the crown
of the Queen of Spain
(who had a daughter)
gold the prize
of your life
the crowning glory
the gateway to heaven
the golden altar
(which I saw in Seville
five hundred years after)

Though I couldn't help noticing
(this filled me with dread):

silver was your armour
silver the cross of your Lord
silver the steel of your countenance
silver the glint of your sword
silver the bullet I bite

Golden the macca
the weeds
which mark our passing
the only survivors
on yellow-streaked soil

We were The Good Indians
The Red Indians
The Dead Indians

We were not golden
We were a shade too brown.

2

At some hotel
overlooking the sea
you can take tea
at three in the afternoon
served by me
skin burnt black as toast
(for which management apologizes)

but I've been travelling long
cross the sea in the sun-hot
I've been slaving in the cane rows
for your sugar
I've been ripening coffee beans
for your morning break
I've been dallying on the docks
loading your bananas
I've been toiling in orange groves
for your marmalade
I've been peeling ginger
for your relish
I've been chopping cocoa pods
for your chocolate bars
I've been mining aluminium
for your foil

And just when I thought
I could rest
pour my own
— something soothing
like fever-grass and lemon —
cut my ten
in the kitchen
take five
a new set of people
arrive
to lie bare-assed in the sun

wanting gold on their bodies
cane-rows in their hair
with beads — even bells

So I serving them
coffee
tea
cock-soup
rum
Red Stripe beer
sensimilla
I cane-rowing their hair
with my beads

But still they want more
want it strong
want it long
want it black
want it green
want it dread

Though I not quarrelsome
I have to say: look
I tired now

I give you gold
I give you the land
I give you the breeze
I give you the beaches
I give you the yellow sand
I give you the golden crystals

And I reach the stage where
(though I not impolite)
I have to say: lump it
or leave it
I can't give anymore

For one day before I die
from the five hundred years of servitude
I due to move
from the kitchen to the front verandah
overlooking the Caribbean Sea
drinking real tea
with honey and lemon
eating bread (lightly toasted, well buttered)
with Seville orange marmalade

I want to feel mellow
in that three o'clock yellow

I want to feel
though you own
the silver tea service
the communion plate
you don't own
the tropics anymore

I want to feel
you cannot take away

the sun dropping by every day
for a chat

I want to feel
you cannot stop
Yellow Macca bursting through
the soil reminding us
of what's buried there

You cannot stop
those street gals
those streggehs
Allamanda
Cassia

Poui
Golden Shower
flaunting themselves everywhere

I want to feel:

you cannot tear my song
from my throat

you cannot erase the memory
of my story

you cannot catch
my rhythm

(for you have to born
with that)

you cannot comprehend
the magic

of anacondas changing into rivers
like the Amazon
boas dancing in my garden
arcing into rainbows
(and I haven't had a drop
to drink – yet)

You cannot reverse
Bob Marley wailing
making me feel
so mellow

in that Caribbean yellow
at three o'clock

any day now.

VEJAY STEEDE

REGGAE...

Wha?? Wha dem say? Dem say dem wan fi know what is reggae? Okay den. Mi haffi tell dem fi true...

Reggae is Afrika humming her favourite tune. Slaves singing as they cut cane in the heart of paradise. Reggae is Two Sevens clashing on the top of a hill. Blue mountains rolling. Calalloo. Chicken back. Reggae is Roots Culture and *Reality*. A *Concrete Jungle* and a utopian vision all rolled into one. *Down Ina de Ghetto*. Reggae is material privation and spiritual opulence. Reggae is schizophrenic. Reggae was born in Afrika and raised in Jamaica... It now lives in St. Ann. Reggae is Rastaman chants over Nyabingi drums. Reggae is Augustus Pablo's flute. Reggae is Rita Marley getting *High, So High*. Ganja. Punny printas. Dancehall. Session...

Reggae is fast living and even faster fighting. Reggae never dies a natural death. *War Ina Babylon*. Reggae is *Police and Thieves* in the street *Burnin' and Lootin'*. RIOT. REVOLT. REVOLUTION!! Reggae is a posse of rude bwoys chanting down Babylon. Rasta philosophy. Selassie I know. Reggae is Nanny, Cudjoe and Paul Bogle chasing *Crazy Baldheads* out of their yard. Leonard Howell preaching about a Blakk King. Alexander Bedward's Blakk wall. Reggae is Blackness at its most beautiful. Shining, sparkling life. BLAKK LIFE. Black Uhuru screaming for *Solidarity!!* Reggae is Steven Biko and Winnie and Nelson Mandela. Reggae is freedom rallyin' round the red gold and green. Reggae is Bob Marley. Bob Marley is Reggae. Ziggy. Reggae is the Wailers wailing songs of freedom on a street corner in Kingston. Reggae has a Black heart. *Soul Fire*. Marijuana brain. Pain. Reggae is struggle. CHAOS. CONFUSION. FIRE and BRIMSTONE burning down Babylon. Remembering Zion. Crying for Zion. A-YAH-WE-DEH. A cultural rebellion. Reggae is a *Soul Rebel*. Peter Tosh's version. Bunny Wailer wailing in *Protest*. Beres *Puttin' up a Resistance*. Reggae lives on the Front Line. Reggae is a *Buffalo Soldier* who never dies in battle. Reggae is IMMORTAL. Reggae never dies…

Reggae is dreadlocks and ital food. Jamaican Patois over dashboard rattling bass. Blakk herb-filled rooms where even the walls are sweating and everything smells Earthy. Reggae is Stone love – the movement. Saxon. Addis. Black Scorpio. Kilamanjaro. Reggae is sound clashes on beaches. Complaining neighbours calling the cops. Ballheads. Reggae worships Jah and longs to be repariated to Ethiopia. *Afrika Must Be Free!* Reggae has *One Love*, humanity. Reggae is universal. Reggae is violent, homophobic and profligate. BOOM BYE BYE IN A BATTY BOY HEAD. Guntalk. Slackness lyrics. Reggae loves Punnany BAD!! *Needle-eye Pum Pum*. Is Reggae misogynist? Maybe, but it will never admit it. Reggae is stubborn and insolent. RUDE. DEFIANT. OBSTINATE. BRAZEN. Reggae is RAW. People who know say that Reggae is *Wicked in a Bed*. Reggae loves a *Rough Wine* and lives for the *Bedwork Sensation*. Reggae is as horny as Hell!! Reggae is somewhat patriarchal.. but da ladies *Ram Dancehall*. Winey Winey. Gyrating Queens seemingly joined at the waist to rock hard rude bwoys exposing their need for love. Rough style. Reggae is Mamfie and Matie and Fatty. Pum Pum shorts on glamorous women. *Sweetness*. Reggae is the original *Bump and Grind*. Reggae is Love. Tough Love. Reggae is Lust. Desire. Primal yearning. FLESH. Reggae is uncontrollable fuck frenzies at the back of the session hall… beside the speakers. Reggae indeed is RAW. VULGAR. BASE. Reggae smells like SEX. Sweet. Natural. EXOTIC. Reggae is Blakk Exotica. Reggae is the chasm between Blakk males and Blakk females. Reggae is also the understanding needed. Reggae is UNITY. BLAKK UNITY. Unity is strength…

Reggae has only one king, but a vast nobility. Reggae smokes a *Chalice in the Palace*. Reggae is URoy, IRoy and the Viceroys. Reggae employs Admirals, Colonels, Generals, Majors, Brigadiers and Lieutenants. Yet Reggae is NOT hierarchical. Reggae is chatting over 12" version sides at your brethren's house when you were thirteen. Reggae is a *Super Ape*. Lee Perry. Lee Perry?? LEE PERRY!! MADNESS. INSANITY. GENIUS!!! Reggae is screaming children and political platitudes. Reggae has a proclivity to

inspire. *FIRE!!* LIGHTAH! LIGHTAH! Reggae is dancehall jug-
glers and *Champion Bubblers*. Reggae is a *Ballistic Affair*. Reggae is
Dangerous. SMART. SHARP. *Cool and Deadly*. Reggae is Jacob
Miller licking weed in a bush. KILLA. Reggae sits in a *Tenement
Yard*, always waiting... never in vain. Reggae is cynical, sarcastic
and facetious. Go ahead and *Laugh Clown*... Reggae will always
laugh last. LAAWD! mi cyaan't tek it no more!! Reggae is Papa San
bawling all the way up the charts. Mad Cobra Flexin' on the
American Music Awards. Ini Kamoze Hot-steppin' all over *Bill-
board*. Patra winin' her way to the top. SHABBA... 'nuff said.
Reggae is the lighter side of sufferation. Reggae can be some funny
shit!! LIFE can be some funny shit... Reggae is LIFE...
   Reggae is US. Reggae is them. Reggae is good. BAD. LIGHT.
DARK. CIVILISED. UNCIVILISED. STRONG. WEAK. Reggae
embraces difference... except Maamba Men. Reggae is not Euro-
pean... but Reggae does not fear Europe... or think that it is
backward, barbaric or inferior. Reggae is all-encompassing. UNI-
VERSAL. INTERNATIONAL. Reggae is BIG BOUT YAH!! Reg-
gae breaks all chains. Demolishes borders. Reggae is non-con-
formist. Reggae has NO LIMITS. Reggae is the West Indies Test
Cricket team dominating the World. Reggae cannot be domi-
nated. Reggae always breaks free. Reggae is FREEDOM. Reggae
is the Maroons. The Caribs. The Arawaks. Reggae is BOUKMAN.
TACKY. CUFFEE. BUSSA. Reggae is Nat Turner, Sam Sharpe
and Harriet Tubman. Reggae is *The Lion of Judah* breaking every
chain. Reggae is Walter RODNEY Grounding with his brothers in
Jamaica. Reggae is remembering Walter. Reggae is Michael Smith,
Kamau Brathwaite, Aime Cesaire and Derek Walcott giving
paradise a voice. REGGAE IS PARADISE'S VOICE!! Reggae is
HAPPINESS. Reggae is misery. Reggae was banished from Guy-
ana in 1980. Reggae will NEVER be defeated by censorship.
WICKEDNESS. INIQUITY. Reggae is resilent. PERTINACIOUS.
PERSISTENT. DEXTEROUS. Reggae got SKILLZ! Reggae AL-
WAYS WINS...
   Reggae is *Number One*. The *Cool Ruler* of the dance. *Uptown Top
Rankin!* Strictly ROOTS. STYLE & FASHION. WHEEL OUT!!

WHEEL OUT!! Rewind selecta! Reggae is a *Rumour* that started in the ghetto. A *Universal Tribulation* that started in a cave. A *Black Liberation Struggle* that started in Zion. A *Night Nurse* who soothes the sufferer's warwounds. Gregory Isaacs. Reggae is longevity. Gregory Isaacs. Reggae is singing hit songs. Gregory Isaacs. Reggae is a Burning Spear through the heart of Babylon. Armagideon. Reggae is eternity. Purgatory. Heaven. Hell. Reggae is eternal damnation for all Downpressors. Emancipation for all slaves. TRUE EMANCIPATION! DE-COLONISATION!! MARCUS SEY. Reggae is Malcolm X, Martin Luther King and Marcus Garvey. Marcus Garvey. *Marcus Garvey*. BLACK STAR LINER. Reggae is going home to ZION. By the *Rivers of Babylon*. Reggae is Max Romeo *Chasing the devil out of Earth*. Reggae is Michael Rose, Puma Jones and Ducky Simpson guessing *Who's Coming to Dinner*. Reggae is slavery. Do you remember the *Days of Slavery*? Ackee and saltfish. Reggae is Ivan fighting to survive in Shantytown. Jimmy Cliff coming HARD!! *Country Boy*. Reggae is the Heptones pleading for a *Fat Girl*. Leroy Sibbles singing sweet. Reggae is Wet Dreams and *Peeny Peeny*. OVER DE *DICKIE* DE GIRLS DEM GONE MAD!! Reggae asks what *One Dance* can do and poses the perennial question: What a *BAM BAM!!* Reggae ina de area MURDERA!! WICKED. HEARTICAL. IRIE. ITES!!

Reggae is J.C. Lodge making Love over her Telephone line. With Shabba. Reggae is Tommy Cowan dialling Carlene Davis' number... BLAKK LOVE. Reggae is Marcia Griffith's singing for as long as she lives... FOREVER. Reggae is Judy Mowatt calling all *Afrikan Children*. STIRRIN' IT UP! Reggae is Django returning to upset the nation. Reggae is *Dis Poem*... Mutabaruka being BLAKK. BRILLIANT. BEAUTIFUL. Reggae is Dennis Brown *Sitting and Watching* the youth, like an old Afrikan sage. *Wake The Town* and tell the people. Reggae is John Holt, Big Youth and Ken Boothe. The Ethiopians, The Jamaicans, The Kingstonians and The Abyssinians. *NOBODY MOVE, NOBODY GET HURT*. Reggae is Yellow, Red, Blakk, Blue, *Young, Fresh and Green*. Reggae is *Puppy Love*... Singing Sweet melodies for *Carol*. Pam. SARAH. SANDRA-SANDRA. Reggae is Lady Saw cuttin' up the weak lovin' man. NONONO...

she don't love me any more. Reggae is Blakk Love unbound. Liberated. Uninhibited. FREE...

Reggae is *Natural Mystic* blowing through the air. LIVITY. Reggae is *Zion In A Vision*. Garnett Silk lives inside Reggae. *Hello Mama Afrika*... Reggae loves you. Reggae is TRAGEDY. DEATH. TEARS. STRIFE. ETERNAL LIFE. Reggae is *Tougher Than Tough*. *Blood and Fire*. Peter Tosh wouldn't be a legend if he hadn't died at the hands of gunmen. Think about it. Reggae is REAL. Real pain. Real death. Real sufferation. Reggae is the song of the sufferers. The fear in the heart of the *Downpressor Man*. Reggae can clearly see *Who The Cap Fit*. Reggae is BURNIN', EXODUS and UPRISING. *Songs of Freedom*. Reggae is the realm where ghetto legends live. Reggae is Bob Marley. BOB MARLEY IS REGGAE. Reggae is politics. Marley joining hands with Michael Manley and Edward Seaga in a show of Unity. Unity is strength. AFRIKAN UNITY. Reggae is the United Negro Improvement Association. The Organisation for AFRIKAN UNITY. Reggae is Pan-Africanism. Reggae is C.L.R. James, George Padmore and W.E.B. Dubois. Reggae is Kwame Nkrumah, Franz Fanon, Patrice Lumumba and Amilcar Cabral. FREEDOM FIGHTERS. Reggae is Che Guevara, Toussaint L'Ouverture, Jean-Jaques Dessalines and Fidel. Reggae is Haiti... Reggae is Cuba. VIVA LA REVOLUCION!! Reggae is dying for the people... Reggae is hot-tempered. Volatile. Reckless. Reggae destroys rude bwoys and builds AFRIKAN MEN. REVO-LUTIONARIES. Reggae is insurgent. Subversive. Seditious. Reggae is an insurrection... It has the spirit of Morant Bay. Reggae loves a good fight. WAR. Reggae has a hard, HARD... Blakk, BLAKK skin, and a VERY sharp tongue. Reggae is Vitriolic. Bitter. Caustic. Vituperative. Spitting daggers of condemnation at the workers of iniquity. Reggae is the language of the righteous... the citizens of ZION. Reggae is Iron like a Lion in Zion. Reggae despises *Babylon System* because it separates humanity. Reggae knows that humanity in One Blood and that only *Time Will Tell*...

Reggae is DUB... DEEP. DARK. BOTTOMLESS. WOOFER BLOWIN' DUB. Reggae is the World in dub. EASTMAN DUB. KUSH DUB. NUBIA DUB. MESAPOTAMIA DUB. FLASH IT!!

Reggae is a perpetual drumbeat that gets into your bones and never leaves. DUB that gets into your muscles and don't let go 'til you're exhausted from SKANKIN' all night. *One Foot Skank*. Reggae is the sound of the wind blowing across AFRIKA. Reggae is the rhythm of stampeding wildebeeests... the cacophony of life on the Serenghetti. Reggae is the call of the Wild. The subtle nuances of nature's song. Reggae is NATURE. Reggae is HUMANITY. Reggae is Nature and Humanity in constant interaction. SATTA AMASSA GANNA. Reggae is race — What the fuck is race anyway?? Capitalist BULLSHIT!! Reggae is not capitalism or communism. Reggae is HUMANism. Reggae hates colonialist SHITSTEMS. Colonialism. Reggae writes and tells its own narrative! BUDDA-BI-BI-BI... BUDDA-BI-BI-BI-BI-BIIE-BIIE!!! Reggae is noises. Sounds. Words that transcend societal barriers and challenge stereotypes. Reggae is positive. Progressive. Radical. Reggae is a language. The language of the ghetto. Reggae is SLENG-TENG... Reggae is LYRICS. Liberating lyrics. Profound lyrics. Enslaving lyrics. Poignant lyrics. 'Nuff 'Nuff Lyrics. Lyrics flowing like the River Nile. Reggae is DJs. Djs chattin' lyrics forever. Reggae is Prince Jazzbo, Jah Lion, Dennis Alcapone and Dr. Alimantado. Reggae is Dillinger, Eek-a-Mouse, John Wayne, Josey Wales and Peter Metro. Reggae is a *Hundred Sexy Girls* chasing Yellowman all over Jamaica. Reggae is a dream. Reggae hits the subconscious mind so hard it hurts. *AGONY*. Reggae is Pinchers. Reggae is Pliers. Reggae is Chaka Demus and Pliers. Reggae is Michigan and Smiley, Rappa and Tippa, Steelie and Clevie. Reggae is Major Mackeral, Major Worries, Tippa Irie and Clement Irie. Reggae is Ranks, Runks, Banton and Daddy. TIGER IN DE DANCE IS A **BAM BAM!!!** Reggae is Pampido, Terror Fabulous, Mega Banton and Bajja Jedd. Reggae is SuperCat, Junior Cat, Top Cat and Snaggapuss. Si *BOOPS* Deh. Reggae is Shelley Thunder. *KUFF!!* Reggae is Sister Nancy, Sister Carol, Lady G and Charmaine. Remember Dignitary Stylish?? DAS REGGAE!! Reggae is Culture lyrics. Brigadier Jerry. Charlie Chaplin. Kulcha Knox. Anthony B. Reggae is *Big Belly Man* who WAN' PUNNANY!! Reggae is Admiral Baily. *JUMP UP! JUMP UP! EV'RY POSSE JUMP UP-UP!!* Reggae is

Nicodemus, Cutty Ranks, Red Dragon, General Trees and Spragga Benz. FRESH!! Reggae is pure, unadulterated, undiluted, ghetto poetry. HARD. COLD. NAKED. REAL. Reggae is the way the ghetto eats, sleeps, breathes. THINKS. SPEAKS. EXISTS. Reggae is Dubified, Sensi-fied, lyrical, poetical ghetto sustenance...

Reggae is Prince Far I. Blakk Reggae music is like a *Message From The King*. REGGAE IS RAS TAFARI MAKONNEN. HAILE SELASSIE I... King of kings, Lord of Lords and the Conquering Lion of the Tribe of Judah. Look to the East for the coming of a blakk King. Reggae has a *Kingly Character*. Reggae is at home in SHASHEMANELAND. Reggae is ignorant. Reggae is insensitive to the plight of the Ethiopian people under the tyranny of Haile Selassie I. Reggae believes in the divinity of Haile Selassie I. Reggae is foolish. FANTASY. MYTH. Reggae explodes myths. Reggae is History. OURstory. *Black MY Story!!* Reggae hates Rome and longs to see it burned to the ground. *NO MORE SODOM AND GOMORRA*. Reggae Gets Flat. HIGH. *RED*. Reggae religiously heeds the *Commandment of Drugs*. Reggae is *AFRIKAN HERBSMEN* being lifted to the next meta-physical dimension. Serious Reasoning. Reggae is sexist. Reggae is escapist. Reggae is consciousness in a world of unconsciousness. Reggae is Ganja laws. *TU-SHENG PENG*. Reggae is illegal. Reggae is despair. NIHILISM. DESPERATION. SUR-VIVAL. Reggae is a *Rat Race*. A hustler. A dealer. A gambler. A street warrior. Reggae is a *Stalk of Sensimilla* growing in the back yard. TU-TU-TWAY. *Call the Police For Me*... But *What De Hell Police Can Do??* Reggae adheres only to the law of Nature. Survival of the fittest. Dog eat dog. Kill or be killed. Only the strong survive. Reggae is STRONGG. Rough Rugged and RAW!! Did I already say Reggae was raw? IT IS!!

Reggae is *Beautiful Mother Nature*. EARTH. AIR. FIRE. WATER. Reggae is Creation. Reggae is the Sun, the Moon, the Stars and the Earth. Reggae is young like sunrise... and old like time. Reggae is a bastard child. Reggae bleeds from its mother's heart and speaks with its father's tongue. *YUSH*. Reggae is a pidgin language. A pidgin culture. DISOWNED. LOST. CONFUSED. AMBIGU-OUS. Reggae is a hybrid son of History. A Mulatto. Bastardised on

a ship and redeemed through the glory of Nature. Reggae is Glory.
PRIDE. BLAKK PRIDE. Reggae is Blood, Sweat and Tears. Reggae
is VICTORY... the victory of good over evil. Reggae is MUSIC... the
sounds of Nature. SWEETSWEETREGGAEREGGAEMUSIC.
Reggae is the sweetest voice on the face of the Earth singing over
a bassline of pure THUNDER... Floor moving, Earth shaking
RIDDIM!! Reggae is *Bass Culture*. 'NUFF RESPECT!! Reggae is
SWEET! Honey. Molasses. Sugar cane. Sticky like a ripe mango.
Delicious like coconut water... jerk chicken... curry goat and
rice... oxtail. Reggae is exquisite. Indulgent. Decadent. Carnivo-
rous. GREEDY. Reggae is materialistic. Grandiose. Beautiful.
Extravagant... like Nature.

Reggae is production. TIGHT. CRISP. SHARP... Razor sharp!
Reggae is riddims on top a riddims. Styles upon styles upon styles.
Reggae is Coxsone Dodd, Duke Reid, Prince Buster and King
Tubby. Reggae is Rockers... ORIGINAL ROCKERS. Augustus
Pablo. Niney, Joe Gibbs, Bunny Lee and King Jammy's. Reggae is
innovation. Experimentation. Reggae is Lee Perry and all his
friends jammin' in the Black Ark. Scratch? SCRATCH!! LU-
NACY. ABSURDITY. *GENIUS!!* Reggae is generations, traditions,
Histories of EXCELLENCE. Reggae is Rico's trombone, Family
Man's bass, Sly's drumstix, Steelie's synthesiser and Dean's sax.
Reggae is Bobby Digital. Sly and Robbie's international acclaim.
Reggae is Desmond Dekker, Derrick Morgan, Joe Higgs and
Delroy Wilson setting standards of excellence... Leroy Smart,
Junior Murvin, Sugar Minott and Freddie McGregor reinforcing
those standards... Barrington Levi, Wayne Smith, Cortney Melody
and Frankie Paul maintaining those standards... And Sanchez,
Beres Hammond, Everton Blender and Luciano carrying those
standards into the 21st century. Reggae is HARMONY. MELODY.
Succulent food for the ear, the mind and the soul. Reggae is The
Melodians, The Mighty Diamonds, The Wailing Souls and the
Starlights. Reggae is *Funky Kingston*. Toots. The Maytals. Reggae is
one big road with *Lots of Signs*. Long live Tenor Saw. Long live Nitty
Gritty. Reggae is Third World, The Gladiators, The Meditations,
Steel Pulse, Israel Vibration and Aswad. Reggae is a *Jezebel*. Justin

Hinds. The Dominoes. Reggae is I JAH MAN, Michel Prophet, Pablo Moses and Junior Reid. Reggae is Home T, Cocoa Tea, Half Pint and Yami Bolo. *Be Still Babylon!!* Reggae is Linton Kwesi Johnson, Yasus Afari, Benjamin Zephaniah and Jean 'Binta' Breeze writing poetry like graffiti across the clean white face of Babylon. Reggae is TALENT... Oodles and oodles and oodles of talent! BLAKK TALENT!!

Reggae is wicked, insane, tongue twistin', fast chattin', *Ragga Ragga* shit that you will NEVER understand if it ain't in your blood. Reggae is SLANG. MYSTERIOUS. ESOTERIC. GHETTO MORSE CODE. SEEN!! Authentic Reggae is NOT AMERI-CANISED. MATERIALISED. CAPITALISED. DILUTED. But sometimes the Americans Bum Rush the Show, like they did in Grenada... That's when you get a Mad Lion. RAGGA-HIP-HOP... a BASTARD genre spawned by two bastard cultures... each one born in the ghetto. Reggae is Born Jamericans. KRS-One chattin' LARGE knowledge. Ice Cube gettin' WICKED. Tony Rebel doing a song with Queen Latifah. Reggae is Public Enemy Fightin' the power... Boogie Down Productions chanting *FREE MUMIA*. Reggae is Mumia Abu-Jamal. Reggae is the MOVE Organisation. Reggae is the Black Panthers. Reggae is Huey P. Newton, Bobby Seale, Elaine Brown, Eldridge Cleaver and Angela Davis. Reggae is Afrika Babbaataa. Reggae is the Zulu Nation. Reggae is NAS puffin' live and representin'. Illmatic. Reggae is being TRUE to yourself, your people and your culture... Reggae is quite comfort-able in the USGhetto. REGGAE IS HIP-HOP...! TRUTH. LOVE. DEVOTION. COMMITMENT. DEDICATION. Reggae demands attention. Affection. Love. Reggae is a RUDE remake of every R&B hit ever written! Reggae is untouchable. WILD. UNRULY. UN-TAMED. Reggae is a jungle... full of Lions and Tigers and reptiles. Reggae is LOUD. VOCIFEROUS. STRIDENT. UNKEMPT. DI-SHEVELLED. RAGAMUFFIN. Reggae don't give a FUCK!! Reggae is XTRA NAKED. COARSE. ABRASIVE. CRUDE. Reggae is **RAW!!** SHABBA... *AS RAW AS EVER*. Reggae is the epitome of rude bwoy angst and ghetto emotionalism. FUCK DA WORLD mentality. PAM! PAM! GUNSHOT IS THE SOLUTION. Ghetto escapism. Ganja clouds. The smell of piss and plantains frying. Reggae *Nah Lef the Dance*. Reggae is rude girl innocence and sound boy machismo. Batty boy condemnation and VIOLENCE. VIOLENCE and more VIOLENCE. Reggae was BOOMBASTIC long before Shaggy arrived. Reggae is spontaneous combustion. HOT. *96 Degrees in the Shade*. Reggae is FIRE burning down Rome. Reggae is *Dread Beat An' Blood*. Reggae is the celebration – glorification – of self-destruction. MURDER. DEATH. TRIBAL WAR. YU DEAD NOW!! Reggae is a clash every night of the year. BRRR... BRRR... BRRRRINNG...BRRRRIINNG... RRRRRIIINNNGG... RING THE ALARM!! Reggae is another sound dying at the stroke of another Jamaican dawn. Reggae is highly competitive. Reggae is the *Best Baby Father*, the *Greatest Girl Lover* and the *Champion Sound*. DON IS DON. Reggae is the Ninjaman/Shabba clash, the Admiral Bailey/Lieutenant Stitchie debate. Reggae is Bounty Killer and Beenie Man sharing the DJ Crown while Capleton and Buju become LEGENDS...

Reggae is *soo* many things. Big things. Small things. EVERYTHING. Reggae is events; Sunsplash, Sting. Reggae is dates; 1865, 1966. Reggae is emotions; Love, anger. Reggae is Memories; *Zimbabwe*, Garnett. Reggae is TIME... time to struggle... time to fight... time to heal... time to love. Reggae is RESISTANCE. RESISTANCE. **RESISTANCE!!** Reggae is strident declarations of Love for AFRIKA and BLAKK existence. Reggae is Tony Rebel shouting his *Nazerite Vow* at the World. *The World Should Know*. Reggae is creativity at its most creative. Reggae is a *Redemption Song*... Reggae is a seed. ROOTS so deep they touch the Earth's core. Reggae is HYPNOTIC. QUIXOTIC. MYSTICAL. MAGICAL. MYTHICAL. Reggae is ANANCY always outwitting the omnipotent Babylonians. Reggae is Buju Banton's conversion to Rastafari. Reggae is the endless pursuit of Peace, Love, Unity and Perfection. Reggae is far more than this poem can say... Reggae is Perfection.

BOB STEWART

AUGUST TOWN

Up from the valley
one night
came a bass-sound darkness
and a treble of light.

Delroy and Pam
and Sheila and Sam
found a peace
beating against
the walls of their valley
the walls
of their flesh

as a timeless trumpet
scatta scatta scattered
the winds in their mind
and cleared the sky
in their belly.
The valley that night
was a chalice of music
dissolving the malice
of day heat

as the voices sang   Stop, children.
Watch this sound.
Take her and hold.
Dance out resistance.
Before these valley walls fold.

WORDS IS NOT ENOUGH
(for Mikey, 1954-1983)

Dem say too many words mad him.
Dem say too many words
bubble up like acid
fi corrupt him mind,
or dat him toss up
word word word
like duppy throw stone
and dem come down back
upon him head.
But what mad him not words.
"Words is not enough,"
him write I.
What mad him was what him see
and him hear
dat was too much fi bear
dat was too much fi word dem.
Him see:
ambassadors of poverty –
him hear:
folly formality –
see scorpion in him dreams,
hear yu curse yu blackness,
see orange fire burn di youth,
hear mother pray fi pickney life –
see yu blind eye
to what him see,
hear yu talk fi stop yu ear
to what him hear.

Is what him see
and what him hear
and what him feel
become a weight

fi bow him down
bring him low
till him hafi limbo
through tunnel so dark
sometime him feel
is only him exist.
Him crawl and him bawl
till him   jus about
fi come out,
him jus right
fi taste di light,
upon di other side –

when stone stone
stone sharp hard stone
stone from de road
him trod under him load
stone from di hand
of di political duppy dem
come down upon him head
before him journey done.

But we nah mourners,
as him say,
we naw guh watch him
wither pon di road.
See him yah
him still deh yah
and watch out:
him word word word
will come down
upon all a we head –

not fi kill
but fi tell
dat words still not enough.

NORMAN WEINSTEIN

DRUMMOND'S LOVER SINGS THE BLUES

A blues begins to moan in her stomach never quite full. Enough.
A moan belongs to her throat/ but throat forbids such transparency. So it starts at her mid/ section/ rises to her lungs as threnody.
A thread of song about wanting babies. But no babies she was. Is.
Babies with no piercing night wails, a utopian grandma model.
Grand design falling unreckoned upon lover's ears, elsewhere. All
stomach between ears and cock. His soon-to-be-born hit song
static on her radio/ kick it into silence since he doesn't listen to her
hit. But her emerging song stops him from tasting her home
cooked dinners. But her appetite drives her to stuff herself with
sweets even after midnight/ so her conception dreams stay sweet.
His dreams reduce her possible-child to rat scurrying under bed/
sheets. Knowing this, she invents a new lover construction fellow
good with hands needling her to conceive by letting go in his
sandpaper embrace. She does. But doesn't leave Drummond tho
daily promises to do so. Which is why she can't really get into
singing the blues, why he sung moans don't soar/ then kamikaze-
dive like frigatebirds at the landfill. Compassion for her plight?
Then be like Jonah & swim into entrails of her singing voice, float
on her hum, move like a long black snake, shape of somebody's
unwanted child. Hers? Feed on her ambivalent pregnancy as if
picking at manna but watch yourself because her lover is picking
up a carving knife watch his moves he's carving a G-clef now on her
belly & as he sinks it in deeper in madness it's his blues drowning
out hers & you're blessed if you get out with your womb of
imagination intact.

Like Kid Ory shadow-boxing with Louie Armstrong
so with saxophonists Tommy & Alphonso, Drummond
blasts his trombone lines into de
militarized zone saxes set up/

:at a check-point
same one used to be in Germany Korea Vietnam
be welcome at the place where you can declare
utter meaning
lessness of possessions/

where only spirit voices
get taken into account
no
one
's counting

& Drummond's pumping brass to keep
the line
moving

GARVEY'S HEAD AS VALUE

                              poisoned wheat let
                    loose at distribution
            points north heads west
                          leaving in its
            wake dozen dead children —
                                                a post
                    election re
            flection fingering
                          a soggy crust at a rum stand —
            incapable of shedding

                          picture of child biting
                    into sandwich of minute
                                    lizard bones —

   interrupted at the Red Star Bakery
as a stranger's hand fills mine with coins

                    cold to touch, didn't
                 check for correct change &

                         too
                         few
                         Garvey
                         heads

                         too
                         late

_____

        done dug up Garvey's
        skeleton from over there

        & planted here like the
        government cares, right?

        nobody's gonna fly this
        skeleton back overseas

        this dread gonna be so full
        of holes there'll be more nothin

        in my grave than in all them
        droopin Ethiopian bellies

        Garvey would've dug roots
        of this mess he's still got

        mighty powerful bones
        & betcha that skull you could

toss like a weapon kick
it whole way to merica

where you can bet
ain't gonna bury those bones

there
ain't no mighty tongued dead

wanna live there
where nobody listens at graves

Build a scale upon tones
of lies about
Zion/Eden, Hit every
note until each echoes

like bird/song when
flock comes up against
Hiroshima-cloud. Start
over. Take a new drum

or horn & try in
venting a scale where
each note a trusted
lover's tender

orgasmic wail. Make
of her ecstasies an
easy Religion. Try
to reach further. Hold

an image of a horn
man playing before
ruins of Neruda's "All
for Art's Sake" mansion

sending herons onto Saint
Marley's rock
steady dance floor. Watch
their flickering body

English. Drummond's
practising a scale
created by stomping
oxen parading in lines

as long as the epic
lies (lines) trailing
the wake of the Santa
Maria. All scales may be

child's play – but this
one heals utter
thing greed. Even stops
lust for the perfect

fantasy of a Fabergé gold egg
a man of taste
would die
for

THE ETHIOPIAN APOCALYPSE OF DON

Their souls parchment dry, brittle, they came
to Don, penniless, hungry, violently
crazed, & said to him: "Help Us!" & he

with nothing but music & madness
shared both generously. & there was
enough for multitudes. Then one

woman who had slept with many of the most
dire stretched out her hand toward
Don, tugging his sleeve. "Is this

carnival silencing your nagging desires?"
Answered by taking her into his hut &
fucking her until the musical soundtrack

to his madness became hers. & crowds
gathered outside his hut waiting for
the couple to peer through the curtain, a

sign the sister had been healed. Three
days passed & no curtain stirred. All left
but a youth who with camel-like affection

followed Don from cafe to cafe. On the 4th
day the couple peered thru the curtain each
wrapped in bloody bedsheets & the boy, unable

to think of what else to utter, shouts: "Are
you healed?" & they, statue-still don't
respond so the youth repeats the question &

with silence following turns to leave &
intuition snaps his neck into looking back:
they're contorting their faces so Don becomes

her & she Don & then she mounts him from
behind, their sheets fallen away, & in high-
soprano he shrieks, giggles, gags. So the boy

came to distrust all apparent (parents')
spiritual & sexual contradictions, distrusting
obvious surface outlines. So he lost

"sin" & learned bondage as a novice
singer for the first time a wobbly note a
wrong pitch waiting

for the perfect arabesque to make
that wrongness an ex
quisite scripture to live by rote

THE MIGRATION OF DRUMMOND'S ORGANS
(AFTER DEATH

lips to the already dead Ayler

good-natured belly to Sonny Rollins

liver (for prophecy) to already dying Marley

hands

?

no one's earned their moves − − *yet*

rest/gods have scattered among anonymous
poor of Trenchtown Jonestown Harlem Bronx

the soul

can not be publicly spoken of/it speaks for itself

Fat Tuesday

Summer solstice

apocalypse

(independence)

day

& thru this dead man's

ears you hear it

with ever increasing speed

arriving

CONTRIBUTORS

John Agard was born in Guyana in 1949. He has lived in Britain since 1977. He has worked as a features writer, librarian and is now a full time writer and performer. In addition to his books for children, his publications include *Limbo Dancer in Dark Glasses*, *Man to Pan*, *Mangoes and Bullets*, *Lovelines for a Goat-born Lady, From The Devil's Pulpit, Half-Caste & Other Poems* and *We Brits*.

Lillian Allen moved from Jamaica to North America in 1969. After studying in New York and Toronto she emerged as a birth mother of dub in Canada, performing at countless events. She has three albums for adults and one for children, two collections of poetry, *Women Do This Every Day* and *Psychic Unrest*, and two books for children and young people. A cultural worker and arts activist in Toronto, Lillian Allen is also a writer of plays and short fiction and is involved with film-making.

Edward Baugh was born in 1936 in Jamaica. He is a poet, critic and professor in the Department of English, UWI in Jamaica. He is the author of *Derek Walcott: Memory As Vision: Another Life*. His poems have been collected in *A Tale From the Rain Forest* and *It Was the Singing*.

James Berry was born in Jamaica in 1924 and has lived in Britain since 1948. He is the editor of two important anthologies of Caribbean and Black British poetry, *Bluefoot Traveller* and *News From Babylon*. His own poetry collections include *Fractured Circles*, *Chain of Days*, *When I Dance, Hot Earth Cold Earth* and *Windrush Songs* from Bloodaxe.

Marion Bethel was born in Nassau in 1953. She is a poet and novelist and feminist activist. Her collection of poems, *Guanahani, Mi Amor*, won the Casa de las Americas prize in 1994. *Her Hurricane of Desire* is due from Peepal Tree in 2009.

Kamau Brathwaite was born in Barbados in 1930. He is a poet, novelist, historian, critic, editor (Savacou) and bibliographer. He taught for many years at the University of the West Indies in Jamaica, but now teaches at New York University. His poetry collections include *Other Exiles*, *The Arrivants* (*Rights of Passage, Masks, Islands,*) *Mother Poem*, *Sun Poem*, *X-Self*, *Blacks & Blues*, *Middle Passages*, *Words Need Love Too*, *Barabajan Poems*, *Golokwati*, *Ark* and *Born to Slow Horses*. His critical study, *Love Axe/*l is at last shortly to be published by Peepal Tree. He is undoubtedly the most significant maker of post-colonial Caribbean culture.

Jean Binta Breeze was born in Jamaica in 1956. She worked as a teacher before training at the Jamaica School of Drama. She is internationally known for her poetry performances. Her publications include *Answers* (1983), *Riddym Ravings* (1988), *Spring Cleaning* (1992) and *On the Edge of An Island* (1997), *The Arrival of Brighteye & other Poems* and *The Fifth Figure*. Recordings of her work include *Riddym Ravings* and *Riding on De Riddym* (1997).

Stewart Brown was born in Southampton in 1951. He has taught in Jamaica, Nigeria and Barbados and is currently at the Centre for West African Studies, the University of Birmingham. He edited *Caribbean New Wave* and *Caribbean New Voices I* and co-edited *Voiceprint*, *Caribbean Poetry Now* and *The Heinemann Book of Caribbean Poetry*. He is a poet in his own right with *Zinder, Lugard's Bridge* and *Elsewhere* (Peepal Tree).

Afua Cooper is a Jamaican-born poet of African descent, living and practising the art of poetry in Toronto, Canada. Her published poetry includes *Memories Have Tongue*, (runner-up for the 1992 Casa de las Americas prize), and *Copper Woman & Other Poems*. Her work seeks to integrate the inner and outer worlds, and combines a sense of history and place with a strong feminist consciousness. She is co-author of *Essays in African-Canadian Women's History* (University of Toronto, 1994).

Fred D'Aguiar was born in London, but raised in Guyana. He has worked as a poet, critic and dramatist. His first collection of poetry, *Mama Dot* (1985), won a number of prizes. It was followed by *Airy Hall* (1989), *British Subjects* (1993), *Bill of Rights* (1998), *Bloodlines* (2000) and *An English Sampler: New & Selected Poems* (2001).

Kwame Dawes was born in Ghana in 1962. He moved to Jamaica in 1971 where he remained until 1987. He has also lived in England, Canada and, currently, America, where he is Professor of English at the University of South Carolina. A one time reggae musician, he has published eleven collections of poetry: *Progeny of Air* (Peepal Tree and winner of the Forward Poetry Prize for best collection of 1994), *Resisting the Anomie* (Goose Lane Editions, 1995), *Prophets* (1995) *Requiem*, *Jacko Jacobus* (both 1996) and *Shook Foil: A Collection of Reggae Poems* (1997), *Midland* (2000), *New & Selected Poems* (2002), *Wisteria* (2006), *Gomer's Song* (2007) and *Impossible Flying* (2007).

Ramabai Espinet was born in Trinidad in 1948. She has lived in Canada for many years where she currently works as a lecturer in Toronto. She is a poet, writer of fiction, essayist and the editor of *Creation Fire*, an anthology of Caribbean women's poetry. Her own collection of poems, *Nuclear Seasons*, was published in 1991, her novel *The Swinging Bridge*, in 2003.

Lorna Goodison was born in Jamaica in 1947. She has published several collections of poetry, including *Tamarind Season* (1980), *I am Becoming My Mother* (1986), *Heartease* (1989), *Selected Poems* (1992), *To Us All Flowers are Roses* (1995), *Turn Thanks* (1999), *Guinea Woman* (2000), *Travelling Mercies* (2001), *Controlling the Silver* (2005) and *Goldengrove* (2006). Her volume of short stories, *Baby Mother and the King of Swords* was published in 1990.

Kendel Hippolyte still lives and writes in his native St Lucia. He has published four collections of poetry, including *Birthright* (Peepal Tree, 1997) and *Night Visions*. He has been described by *The Heinemann Book of Caribbean Poetry* as 'perhaps the outstanding Caribbean poet of his generation'. His work has also been anthologised in *The Penguin Book of Caribbean Verse*, *Voiceprint*, *Caribbean Poetry Now*.

Audrey Ingram-Roberts was born in Jamaica and lives in the Bahamas. She has written and published poetry for several years while working as a management training consultant. Her work has appeared in a number of anthologies, including *Creation Fire*.

Bongo Jerry was one of the first Rastafarian poets to have a major impact on the radicalisation of Caribbean poetry in the early 1970s. He was published in the celebrated *Savacou 3/4* and *Abeng*, and anthologised in *Voiceprint*.

Linton Kwesi Johnson is known and revered as the world's first major dub poet. A committed performer, his recordings span two decades, the most recent album being *LKJ A Capella Live*. His poems first appeared in *Race Today*, and were quickly followed by three publications, *Voices of the Living and the Dead* (1973), *Dread Beat and Blood* (1975) *Inglan Is A Bitch* (1980) *Tings an' Times: Selected Poems* (Bloodaxe, 1991), *Mi Revalueshanary Fren* (2002) and *Selected Poems* (2006).

Jane King is a St Lucian teacher and writer and a founding member of the Lighthouse Theatre. Her stories and poems have appeared in a number of Caribbean journals and anthologies, including *Confluence: Nine Saint Lucian Poets*. Two of her own collections of poetry have been published: *In to the Centre* and *Fellow Traveller* which was awarded the James Rodway Memorial Prize by Derek Walcott.

Dorothy Wong Loi Singh was born in Suriname. She works in adult education. She is a painter and her poetry has been published in a number of journals and anthologies, including *Creation Fire*.

Malachi was born in Westmoreland, Jamaica. He was one of the founding members of 'Poets in Unity', an ensemble which brought dub poetry to the forefront of Reggae in the late 70s and carried it forward for a decade. Malachi has performed as an actor and poet, and has become known for his performances on radio, television and live theatre. He was 'Dub Poet of the Year' at 1995's ReggaeSoca Awards.

Anthony McNeill was born in Jamaica in 1941. He died in 1996. He was widely recognised as one of the most original of the generation of poets following Brathwaite and Walcott. He was among the first Caribbean poets to explore images of reggae and Rastafarianism in his work. His collections include *Hello Ungod* (1971), *Reel From 'The Life Movie'* (1972), and *Credences at the Altar of Cloud* (1979).He won the 1995 Jamaica National Literary award with his *Chinese Lanterns from the Blue Child* which was published by Peepal Tree in 1998.

Ahdri Zhina Mandiela was born in Jamaica and now lives in Toronto. She is a theatre artist and performance dub poet. She concentrates much of her literary and stage work in the public school system. She is involved in such community organs as Black Meres (a Black mothers anti-racism collective). Her publications include *Special Rikwes* and *Dark Diaspora in Dub*.

Rachel Manley was born in England, of an English mother and a Jamaican father, but came to Jamaica at the age of two. She grew up with her grandparents, N.W. Manley, leader of Jamaica's nationalist move-ment, and Edna Manley, the sculptor and energetic promoter of Jamaican arts. She is the author of three collections of poetry, *Prisms*, *Poems 2* and *A Light Left On* (Peepal Tree Press, 1992).

Marc Matthews is a Guyanese poet, who worked in broadcasting and drama before moving to London, where he still works as an actor and one-man performer. His first collection of poems, *Guyana, My Altar*, won the 1987 Guyana Prize for poetry. This was followed by *A Season of Sometimes* (Peepal Tree, 1992).

Mbala (Michael Bailey) has been performing poetry in Jamaica since the 1970s, self-accompanied on acoustic instruments including congas, guitar, bamboo flutes and saxophone. He works as a graphic designer and has done set and costume design for a number of Jamaican theatre companies. He has been vice-president of the Poetry Society of Jamaica.

Brian Meeks was born in Canada in 1953, but his family returned to Jamaica in 1956. A political activist in the seventies, he was involved in post independence arts and youth work. Kamau Brathwaite refered to him as one of the new generation of '*brigadista*' Jamaican poets, wielding an 'unwhitened' language. Meek's poems were published in *Savacou* and anthologised in *Voiceprint* (1989). His novel *Paint the Town Red* was published by Peepal Tree in 2003.

Pam Mordecai has worked in her native Jamaica as a teacher, radio and television presenter, producer, critic, and publisher. Her poems have appeared in *Bim*, *Jamaica Journal*, *Savacou* and the *Caribbean Quarterly*, and anthologised in collections such as *The Heinemann Book of Caribbean Poetry*. She is author of *Story Poems* (1987) *Journey Poem* (1989), *De Man* (1995) *Certifiable* (2001) and *The True Blue of Islands* (2005). She is co-editor of *Jamaica Woman*, (1980) and *Her True-True Name* (1989).

Mervyn Morris was born in Jamaica in 1937. He is Reader in West Indian Literature at UWI. He co-edited *Jamaica Woman* (1980), *Voiceprint* (1989), and edited *The Faber Book of Contemporary Caribbean Short Stories* (1990). He worked with Michael Smith on *It a Come* just before the latter's murder. His own collections of poetry include *The Pond* and *Shadow Boxing* (1973), *On Holy Week* (1988), *Examination Centre* (1998) and *Been There, Sort of: New and Selected Poems* (2006).

Grace Nichols was born in Guyana in 1950. She has published children's stories, and a novel, *Whole of the Morning Sky* (1986). She won the Commonwealth Poetry Prize in 1983 for her *i is a long-memoried woman* (1983), which she followed with *The Fat Black Woman Poems* (1984) *Lazy Thoughts of a Lazy Woman* (1989) *Sunris* (1996) and *Startling the Flying Fish* (2006).

Opal Palmer Adisa was born in Jamaica. A literary critic, writer and storyteller, her *Tamarind and Mango Women* (1992), won the pen Oakland/Josephine Miles Award. Her publications include *Pina, The*

Many-Eyed Fruit (1985), *Bake-Face and Other Guava Stories* (1986), *traveling women* (1989), *Leaf of Life* (2000), *Caribbean Passion* (Peepal Tree, 2004) and *Eros Muse* (2007). Her essays were included in *Daughters of Africa* (1992), and *Caribbean Women Writers* (1990). She holds the chair of Ethnic Studies at California College of Arts and Crafts.

Geoffrey Philp was born in Jamaica, educated at Jamaica College and graduated from the University of Miami. He lives and works in Miami. He is the author of three collections of poetry, *Exodus and Other Poems*, *Florida Bound, Hurricane Center* and *Xango Music*, the latter three published by Peepal Tree. His collection of short stories, *Uncle Obadiah and the Alien* was published by Peepal Tree in 1997.

Velma Pollard was born in Jamaica in 1937. She lectures in Language Education at the University of the West Indies. She is the author of two collections of short stories: *Considering Woman*, and *Karl: and Other Stories* and a novel, *Homestretch*. Her collections of poetry, *Crown Point and Other Poems, Shame Trees Don't Grow Here ... but poincianas bloom* and *Leaving Traces* were published by Peepal Tree.

Rohan Preston was born in Jamaica, reared in New York and lives in Chicago. He won the 1997 Henry Blakely, Jr. Poetry Prize, and was awarded an Artist Fellowship in Poetry from the Illinois Arts Council. His poems have appeared in *The Atlanta Review*, *Crab Orchard Review*, *Eyeball*, *Hammers*, *Jackleg* and *Ploughshares*. His poetry collections include *Dreams In Soy Sauce* (Tia Chucha, 1992) and *Lovesong to My Father* (Tallawa). He co-edited *Soulfires: Young Black Men on Love and Violence* (Penguin, 1996).

Lloyd Richardson was part of the explosion of radical, post-colonial writing in Jamaica in the early 1970s. His work appeared in the Savacou *New Poets From Jamaica*. He was born in 1954 and died, tragically young, in 1978.

Dennis Scott was born in Jamaica in 1939. With Brathwaite, McNeill and Goodison, he was one of the first Caribbean poets to reflect the realities of reggae and Rastafarianism in his poetry. Dennis Scott also won acclaim as a playwright, director, critic, actor and dancer. He was principal of the Jamaica School of Drama, and Associate Professor of Directing at Yale University. His poetry collections include: *Journeys and Ceremonies* (1969), *Uncle Time* (which won the 1974 Commonwealth

Poetry Prize), *Dreadwalk* (1982), and *Strategies* (1989). He died in 1991. His *After-Image* is published by Peepal Tree in 2008.

Olive Senior was born in Jamaica in 1941. She lives both there and in Canada. Her first collection of short stories, *Summer Lightning* (1986), won the Commonwealth Literature Prize. She has published two subsequent collections of short stories: *The Arrival of the Snake Woman* (1989) and *The Discerner of Hearts* (1995) She has four published collections of poems: *Talking of Trees* (1985) *Gardening in the Tropics* (1995), *Over the Roofs of the World* (2005) and *Shell* (2008). She has written on different aspects of Caribbean culture, and was editor of *Jamaica Journal*.

Vejay Steede is from Bermuda. Although he sees himself as 'nationless', his work is heavily influenced by West Indian culture, and the likes of Marcus Garvey, Bob Marley and Kamau Braithwaite. He aims to create a space where 'Blakkness may be celebrated without fear or shame.' *Reggae* was his first published poem. He published *Kollage: The Scribblings of an Onion Seed* in 2001.

Bob Stewart was born in New Jersey, USA, but was resident in Jamaica for a large part of his life. He taught in Kingston before working as a tutor at the University of the West Indies, where he acquired a doctorate in history. His poems appeared in a series of Caribbean and international publications, including *Arts Review*, *Jamaica Journal*, *Savacou* and *Race Today*. His own volume, *Cane Cut* was published by Savacou Cooperative in 1988, after his return to the US.

Norman Weinstein is a poet and critic and writer on jazz and reggae. His most recent book is *A Night in Tunisia: Imaginings of Africa in Jazz* (Limelight Editions). His books of poems include *Nigredo* (Station Hill Press), *Algredo* (North Atlantic Books), and *Suite: Orchid Ska Blues* (Mellen Poetry Press).

INDEX OF TITLES

INDEX OF FIRST LINES